This is book No. _23_
of 850 specially numbered
copies of
Rio Grande Memories.

Rio Grande Memories

By John B. Norwood

Edited by Debra Brinkman

Layout by Charis Lehnert

Library of Congress Catalog Card Number:
91-71587

ISBN 0-911581-21-9

First Edition
Printed in United States of America

Heimburger House Publishing Company
7236 W. Madison Street
Forest Park, Illinois 60130

 # Dedication

The Navajo Indians are firmly convinced that "Those Who Went Before" have left behind a mana that can influence their thoughts, life and feelings. This mana is evoked by tribal songs and oral recitations; they have no other means of picturing and recalling their past.

We are more fortunate. As rail aficionados, we are indebted to "Those Who Went Before" with cameras and with almost the same devotion to the "High Iron" as the men who manned the trains running on that rail. They painted the cinders and smoke, the music of well-tuned valves, the dance of counterbalances and siderods, the melody of wheels passing over rail joints, the sound of a far distant steam whistle blowing and the derring-do of those who laid the rail.

This book is dedicated to "Those Who Went Before" and left us tangible images, pictures which, either through experience or vague remembrance, we can relate to: images of a scene, incidents in a time, place or environment that if, not stilled, would have been lost to us forever.

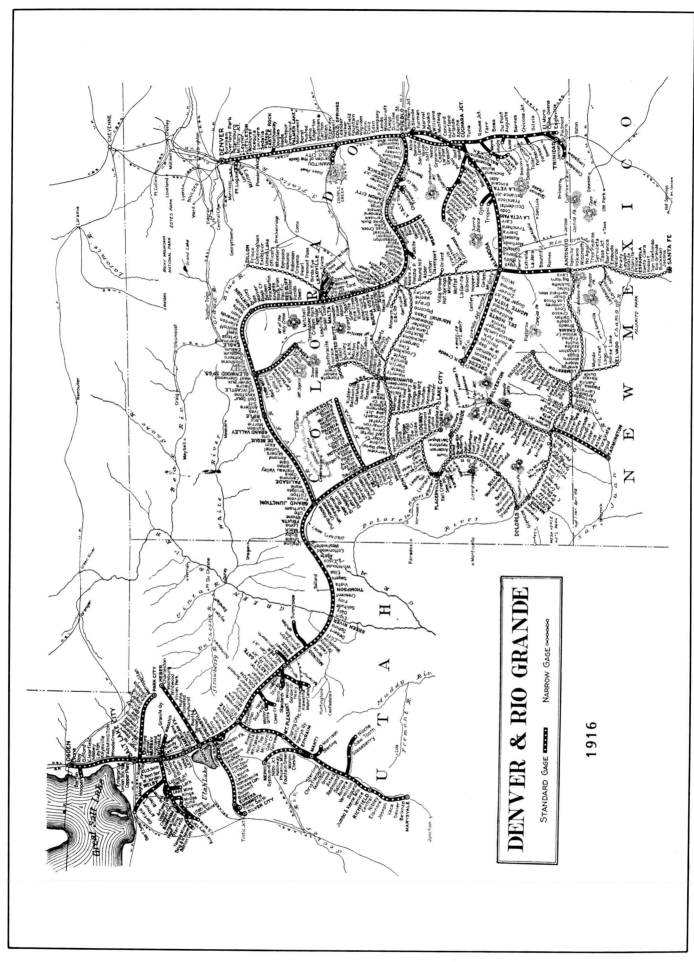

DENVER & RIO GRANDE

STANDARD GAGE ▪▪▪▪▪▪ NARROW GAGE ○○○○○○

1916

4

Contents

Preface

During the winter months when hunting seasons are over and fishing waters are frozen, when you cannot risk old bones on the ski slopes, finding something to do often becomes a problem.

Fortunately, a number of years ago Donald Heimburger challenged me to put some of my railroad experiences in writing. Thinking I had enough notes and photos, I started my first book. How wrong could I be?

Very quickly I found a need for historical data and photos. Employees of the Colorado Historical Society and the Denver Public Library saw me often. Becoming fascinated by the overwhelming amount of material available and the work necessary to gather, catalog and categorize it, I soon became a gratis volunteer at the Society.

Researching the history of the Rocky Mountain Empire during the winter months became a gratifying avocation. Needless to say, my major interest was railroad history and mining. The Colorado Historical Society at Denver has over a half million photos of the general and railroad history of the Rocky Mountain Empire. There are literally tons of collected memoirs and accounts of the building of Colorado and contiguous states.

My observations of the people who come for information and research is almost as intriguing as the materials available. For the most part, they are students preparing thesis, journalists or individuals preparing papers to present to clubs or other organizations. Then there are authors or would-be authors. Most are under 40 years of age. Only occasionally does anyone in my age group appear.

CHERISHING THE PAST

The older people come to research information about a remembered incident or family information. The younger people, it strikes me, seem to share a common consensus that the history of Colorado and the West began somewhere about World War I. On the whole, anything earlier than that is antediluvian. Their tendency is to pore over old newspaper files, journals, magazines and personal memoirs. With that half million photos available, few ask to view them. To me, this is tragic.

The pictures tell so much more; memoirs, newspaper reports, journals, even books and magazine articles can only reflect the writer's view and impressions of history. Future writers, using this material, pass on their interpretations of this material to their readers or audiences. These in turn form their own images and impressions. The end result is that an erroneous understanding of historical matter evolves.

Soon after I was assigned by the Rio Grande to study and make reports on other railroads, I discovered that no matter how hard I tried, or how many words I used, I was not delivering mental images to others as I saw them. Then, I began using cameras. It became a new ball game. Less time was spent at a typewriter, and I was not required to answer as many follow-up questions.

True, pictures can be faked, but you do not find these in collections of photographs by camera users intent only on recording a scene for their own pleasure or memories. Those old photos represent images of people, places, occasions and scenes, preserved for us by the miracle of the camera and film.

THE ROOTS OF FASCINATION

Many—no, most—of the half million pictures donated or collected were taken by amateurs. Not all are of quality suitable for reproduction. But occasionally, while categorizing and cataloging these pictures, I find those that I could almost "walk into." The photographer, either by expertise or accident, captured an image that carries the viewer out of himself/herself. The viewer is transported back in time to experience what the photographer saw, how he felt, and what he admired or was impressed by at the moment he snapped the shutter.

Railroads, their history and operation, have become almost an obsession with those dedicated people known as "railfans." The dominating love of the dedicated is Steam. Maybe some day there will be a cult of railfans who worship diesel engines, but I seriously doubt this. The diesel locomotive, a marvel of technological development, simply lacks the capability of stirring the blood and imagination or creating nostalgia as only a steam locomotive can.

Pictures and stories of railroads in the beginning with the small, simple 18- to 30-ton teakettles, take railfans back to the roots of their fascination. The size of equipment and improvements of plant continue. At last, too few years before dieselization, came the period of steam power when the apogee of railroad fascination was reached and those breathtaking, pulse-stirring sights and sounds of the last generations of steam power were gone. Imagine a blur of speed, the vortex of a sleek, beautiful behemoth of steam power rolling by to the tune of perfectly squared valves and flashing siderods before the eyes. Then, if the wind blew right, one could smell coal smoke filtering through the air. Even the oil burners smelled better than diesel.

In a sense, like the students who date history as beginning with World War I, we shortchange ourselves if we lose contact with the beginnings, the roots, of rail history. Even more, if we do not use photographs to let us see the real thing, we are in danger of losing the real things—time and its mysterious moments.

I am fortunate to have lived and worked on the Rio Grande during the period of transition. I worked on the Narrow Gauge when there were still 30-ton engines being used and on the standard gauge districts when steam engines weighed 675 tons.

As a young boy, I remember my father leaving the D&RGW to go to work on the Rio Grande Southern because Green River, Utah, ceased to be a hub-terminal west of Grand Junction. This was brought about when an ill-advised management decision built a major terminal on the windy, snowy, mountain top at Soldier Summit, Utah. This was at a time when heavy rail weighed 90 pounds-to-the-yard, and the heaviest standard gauge engines were Class F-81s, the 1400s. I saw rail weight increase to 130-pound or heavier, and steam locomotives weighed in at 675 tons. I dispatched trains first by telegraph, then telephones, using train orders, and finally, I dispatched them using CTC and radios.

On the Narrow Gauge (D&RGW and RGS), there was a period when the biggest engines were the K-27s, the 450s-460s, when I saw more trains with C-Class engines on the point than Ks. Finally, I was to ride and dispatch the heavy engines, the K-36 and K-37 Class engines, the 480s and 490s.

COMING INTO FOCUS

I have memories of walking on the top of rails on the Rio Grande Southern on sidetracks and spurs which, without doubt, still had 30- to 40-pound rail in them; memories of people listening spellbound as an old ex-master mechanic told tales of being assigned to working with Westinghouse during the installation and indoctrination of enginemen in the use of automatic air brakes; memories of hobnobbing with a number of train service men with missing fingers—lost when they did not use the wooden paddle in making a link-and-pin coupling.

These are memories to be cherished. Too often, they are nebulous, ephemeral. Writing now of them, reading other accounts, they come into focus. While looking through the thousands of old photographs at the Colorado Historical Society, the focus becomes sharp and the memories become much clearer.

Looking at old pictures of snow-fighting, washouts, floods and picking up wrecks (derailments) on the Narrow Gauge and the standard gauge, I can again experience the bone-chilling cold of the Animas Canyon on the Silverton Branch while clearing snow slides; I can again burn in the sweltering heat of the Utah desert while on a rail relaying job; I can again experience my feet hurting and my eyes aching from a long siege at a wreck that is blocking movements of transcontinental business. Again, there are calls of distress from a stomach too long away from solid food and bloated from too copious consumption of caboose coffee. (Now that trains run without cabooses, will railroads provide a means of making that poisonous brew for crew members?)

No storyteller, no writer, can orally or in written words, create an image that will produce the awe, respect, beauty, understanding or the sense of being there that one photo can capture.

This is not a history book; neither is it a storybook. But, there are pictures that have recalled old scenes, reminiscences of what it was like in the beginning. Essentially, it is a picture book. Pictures that have had the ability to let me close my eyes, leave my body and become one with "Those Who Went Before."

May they do the same for you so that as a railfan you will have a clearer understanding of why you are fascinated and obsessed by the high iron and shiny rails.

John B. Norwood
June, 1991

A Rio Grande steam switcher works the mines at Belden, Colorado about six miles east of Minturn, along the Eagle River. Later, New Jersey Zinc developed a large zinc mining operation here; the company placed all of its operating equipment, machinery and shops in man-made subterranean spaces because of the narrow canyon walls. The company even built a town called Gilman, high above on the plateau. When Belden was in full operation, it was the most difficult location on the railroad to switch and service. *W.H. Jackson photo, Colorado Historical Society*

Chapter 1
William H. Jackson

Because of my addiction to railroads and mines, I keep returning to the folios containing the William H. Jackson Collection.

Railfans by the hundreds, thousands, overrun the world today toting their cameras with camera bags full of lenses and film. This is especially true of the Rocky Mountain areas and the Rio Grande Railroad. These camera buffs have shot feet of elevation off the mountain peaks and fired off such a barrage of film that the railroads must repaint and repair their equipment at the end of each railfan season after the shrapnel of film and the flare of flash equipment has eased.

Few of these fans will ever come close to approaching the quantity and quality work of William H. Jackson, the first railfan with a camera.

Even with our advanced photographic technology, few approach the quality of his pictures made 100 years ago using glass plates and box cameras. The clarity, sharpness and depth of field found in his pictures is incredible.

It is estimated Jackson took about 80,000 pictures of the West, including thousands of railroad pictures. His equipment originally was an 8 x 10" camera, glass plates and chemicals, a tripod and a developing tent that was light proof, which in total weighed 300 pounds. He later used a 12 x 14" camera and eventually used an enormous one of 20 x 24". The weight factor became ever more pronounced. In the earlier years while Jackson was with the F.V. Hayden U.S. Geological Survey, this equipment was carried on a pack mule. In rough country, the mule could not carry it all, and some had to be carried by men.

THE JACKSON SPECIAL

Few of today's railfan-photographers ever have had a faithful helper like Jackson's famous old white mule, Dolly, to carry equipment up mountain sides and down into deep canyons. Nor will they ever be assigned a special train, the *Jackson Special,* with its assigned locomotive, Engine No. 273, a private car and assigned crew, which traveled wherever Palmer and Jackson chose to go on the Denver & Rio Grande, Rio Grande Western and Rio Grande Southern.

None will ever be given a contract by the Union Pacific to take 10,000 pictures along its line. Jackson did have such a contract. It may be doubted that he took this many pictures considering that during this

Studio portrait of William H. Jackson about 1869. *Colorado Historical Society*

William Henry Jackson, 1875 *Colorado Historical Society*

At the left of photo, Jackson's photographic train with Business Car "K" descending into the Arkansas River Valley between Mears Junction and Poncha Springs. Mount Shavano looms in the background, covered in beautiful snow. In those days the Rockies were a vast, untamed territory. *W.H. Jackson, Colorado Historical Society*

This is William Jackson, shown in 1868 preparing to join the Hayden Survey. *Colorado Historical Society*

period, he was using an 8 x 10" camera and glass plates, but he did document the Union Pacific to a saturation point.

Jackson was born in 1843 and died in 1942 at the age of 99. He saw railroads develop from the time of engines such as the D&RG's No. 1, *Montezuma,* 30-pound iron rails and locally hacked ties to huge steamers and diesel-electrics rolling on 136-pound steel rails laid on precisely cut, treated ties and controlled by CTC.

From the perusal of Jackson's papers at the Colorado Historical Society, I cannot find any indication that he was acquainted with Mathew B. Brady, the famous photographer of the Civil War. However, it is evident he was influenced by Brady's work and may have met Brady in 1876 when Jackson spent time giving lectures on photography and showing pictures

This is the summit of Marshall Pass on the Salida-Gunnison narrow gauge route. Construction hadn't yet begun of the covered wye and station facilities; just above snowsheds, a picnic area later was cleared. *W.H. Jackson, Colorado Historical Society*

illustrating the glories of the Western United States at the Philadelphia Centennial Exposition.

OMAHA STUDIO

Jackson opened a studio in Omaha in 1867 to take portraits and was moderately successful. In 1870, he was offered the opportunity to join the F.V. Hayden U.S. Geological Survey. He accepted and performed some work in other areas for Hayden before the Colorado portion began in 1873. In 1871, along with Hayden's party, Jackson photographed Yellowstone National Park. His pictures, and Hayden's reports, were influential in establishing Yellowstone in 1872 as our oldest and largest national park, called the Grand Tetons, originally.

The Colorado Survey began in 1873, and Jackson made memorable pictures of the Mount of the Holy Cross. In 1875, Jackson photographed the Canyon de Chelly ruins, after having taken the first pictures of Mesa Verde in 1874. Jackson spent most of 1876 in the East at the Philadelphia Centennial Exposition. Returning to the West and Hayden, Jackson spent 1877 in the Southwest including Colorado, New Mexico, Arizona and Nevada, during which time the first photographs of note were made of the Grand Canyon.

The field work of the survey for Jackson ended with the Wyoming segment; then in 1879, he opened a portrait studio in Denver. When his assistants became capable of doing the studio work, Jackson turned to railroad photography. A total of 12 years was spent doing this. He took photos of the Union Pacific,

Jackson, at left, packs a mule with his equipment to go where wagons couldn't go on Hayden Survey, 1874. *Colorado Historical Society*

11

Palmer's and Otto Mears' lines as well as many of the other roads that opened in Colorado, Utah and New Mexico. He spent time in 1883 on the Mexican Central, one of Palmer's ventures in Mexico.

His name and fame as a railroad photographer was great, and in 1894, he began a photographic tour of the world.

RETIRES IN 1903

After much world traveling, he returned to Denver and engaged in general photography, retiring in 1903 from all but pleasure traveling, to operate the Detroit Company, under the aegis of which thousands of his plates were reproduced. His photographs were so popular that there was a demand for them to be made into postcards. In order to obtain his pictures, a company bought his studio with all prints for $30,000. He spent from 1903-1940 in semi-retirement writing and taking some pictures.

Some 2,500 of his plates, owned by the D&RGW Railroad, were damaged during a fire. The better images were donated to the Colorado Historical Society. Some of the better views were cracked, but they were of such interest and quality, painstaking efforts were made to restore them.

Jackson was certainly a pioneer. He was the first to use a rubber band-actuated shutter that permitted an exposure of about one-tenth of a second. He took the first photos of the Georgetown Loop. He took a picture of a passenger train bound from Silverton to Durango traversing the high line of the D&RGW above the gorge of the Animas River just west of Rockwood. This photo has been duplicated countless times by other photographers.

Eastman introduced a paper film in 1880 and gelatin film in 1884, both of which could be placed directly in the camera. However, Jackson had no faith in either and continued to take his unforgettable railroad pictures with wet plates, and later, dry plates, which he experimented with until he accepted them. It was late in the 1880s when he accepted Eastman gelatin film.

Name any Rocky Mountain area railroad, proposed or in actual operation between 1880 and 1900, and Jackson walked its rails and photographed its trains.

White Rock Point

As an early day photographer, Jackson had to work with tools (cameras) that were not much further advanced than the hand tools used by the builders of railroads contemporaneous with Jackson.

He also found it necessary to live and eat under the same primitive conditions these builders did. The living conditions were far from comfortable; at times, they were almost unlivable.

A case in point is a photo he took at White Rock Point, later renamed Shepherd's Point, that for many

A Rio Grande freight descends the west side of Marshall Pass with brakemen riding atop the cars. They have their clubs ready to assist the engineer in controlling the speed of the train. Note the cowcatcher in the bottom center of the picture; it is of early wooden construction. *W.H. Jackson, Colorado Historical Society*

For many years White Rock Point shown here was classed as the Colorado-New Mexico state line. A survey to settle the dispute about where the line was, later set the line at about Cresco Siding, a short mile to the west (rail distance). The cabins and shelters were the living quarters for the contractor's crews working the grading. Wolf Creek flows into the rocky canyon to the left of the picture. The Great Osier forest fire did not burn this far west. Note the telegraph pole line; it's truly a pole line, no crossarms yet. *W.H. Jackson, Colorado Historical Society*

years was recognized as being on the Colorado-New Mexico state line. A station, Cresco, was about one mile west of this point. The picture was taken soon after the road had reached Chama, New Mexico.

The dwellings, if they can be so graced, are the relics left behind at a contractor's camp engaged in grading work while the line was being built. They were roughly built from logs cut nearby with sod roofs and there were no windows and only rudimentary chimneys for smoke to escape from fireplaces.

It is possible the building in the lower left corner of the photo served in part as the living quarters and office for a telegraph operator because there is a pole near it and other wires running up to the railroad grade that probably carried telegraph wires.

The two-car train on the track above the cable remains is without doubt a Palmer-Jackson inspection-photographing "Special". Alone or together, Palmer and Jackson traveled many miles over the D&RG as far west as Ogden before Palmer retired as president in 1883.

SAN JUAN EXTENSION

On the San Juan Extension of the Narrow Gauge, there were two tunnels. Tunnel No. 1, the Mud Tunnel, was at Milepost 311.3; Tunnel No. 2, Toltec Tunnel, was at Milepost 315.2. Mud Tunnel was built through a combination of soil and rock that required timbering support of the walls. Toltec Tunnel was blasted through granite and no timbering was needed.

Mud Tunnel offered nothing of the spectacular, but Toltec Tunnel was a different story. It exited at the west end at the edge of a small chasm that led downward to the bottom of Toltec Gorge through which the Los Pinos River flowed several hundred feet below the railroad grade. The view at this point looking down to the river was awesome. (Just across this chasm on a rocky shelf a monument to assassinated U.S. President Garfield was later erected.)

To span this chasm, a structure of wooden timbers was built. It was a good example of how the D&RG builders in the beginning made use of materials to be found in the area. And, it also demonstrated the abilities of carpenters and bridge builders of the day.

Jackson took this picture possibly on the same trip he photographed the cabin remains at Shepherd's Point because the engine posed at the tunnel's exit is the same.

As the railroad matured the timber structure was replaced with a cut stone and steel girder structure that filled the chasm at the point where the track crossed. A culvert opening at the base of this new structure permitted any stream flow or seasonal run-off of melting snow to discharge into the Los Pinos River.

Palmer retired from the D&RG in 1883, but retained ownership of the RGW in Utah. Mining was a major activity in the mountains south of the main line

A train pops out the west portal of Toltec Tunnel on the Cumbres route. A tunneling crew poses on the tender of the locomotive. Because the mountain is granite here, no timber lining is needed. The chasm at the portal is still spanned by a wooden trestle. In a flat, protected area under a cliff at the top center of the picture, was the work crews' camp. As late as 1957, I found rusted black powder canisters and camp remains at the spot. *W.H. Jackson, Colorado Historical Society*

AT RIGHT. All the tunnels in Glenwood Canyon were drilled ahead of the grading of roadbed and laying of rails. Here a construction crew is at the tunnel just west of the present-day Shoshone, waiting for the rails to catch up. *W.H. Jackson, Colorado Historical Society*

The Ophir Loop on the Rio Grande Southern is better known, but Tintic Branch loop in Utah on the Rio Grande can hold its own. Note the fourth train passing beneath trestle. Date is 1905-1910. *W.H. Jackson, Colorado Historical Society*

A mixed train on the same trestle on top and a freight train below; the mixed carries the car *South* at the rear, which was either a Southern Pacific or Southern Utah car that ran from Price, Utah. *W.H. Jackson, Colorado Historical Society*

of the RGW and west of the Marysvale Branch. Much of the activity centered in the Eureka, Utah area.

In 1891-1892, Palmer built a standard gauge branch 39.74 miles long that left the main line at Springville, Utah and went to Eureka, Utah. About 22 miles from Springville at Goshen, Utah, very rough mountainous terrain began. Elevation at Goshen was 4,530 feet; at Eureka, 6,573 feet. This resulted in 14 miles of 3 percent grade and 4 miles of 4 percent grade.

It was a tortuous route that required two tunnels and a number of loops, and one monumental timber trestle. Jackson went to the RGW to do some photographing for Palmer. "Palmer Specials" were no longer being run for Jackson, but he could still ask for and be granted the privilege of posing trains at especially pho-

togenic locations while he took his pictures. The shots made of the great trestle with one train passing under it, the one train on it, and the two other trains on the loops of the hillside beyond are memorable ones.

Railroads being built in the mountains, the Canadian Pacific, Union Pacific, Southern Pacific, Great Northern, Northern Pacific, Rio Grande Western, and the Denver & Rio Grande, often found it necessary to build trestles like this one to shorten mileage across declivities. They all drew on the expertise of mine timbering carpenters including Italians and Mexican stone cutters and masons, and a craft of railroad bridge builders. Their knowledge and expertise were gradually lost as the production and use of steel girders and concrete techniques became more prevalent.

Jackson's photo was taken at a reception in honor of himself on his 94th birthday at Denver. *Colorado Historical Society*

To get from Silverton to Ouray before Otto Mears built the Rio Grande Southern, one had to traverse this dangerous wagon road. *W.H. Jackson, Colorado Historical Society*

Chapter 2

Famous Stations on the D&RG

Salt Lake City Union Station

In 1883, Salt Lake City, Utah welcomed the coming of the Denver & Rio Grande to provide competition and, hopefully, lower freight and passenger rates on the Union Pacific. The community also anticipated that this competition would provide improved service.

The bitter rivalry between the UP and the D&RG did produce some improvements. However, this rivalry also kept the two antagonists from accepting the sensible action of building a large joint depot for the use of passenger trains. They refused to construct one together. Each, in trying to outdo the other, overbuilt and, consequently, was saddled with unnecessary maintenance and operating costs.

The D&RG was the major route from Salt Lake City to Denver via Grand Junction, Colorado. Just a few years after it arrived in Salt Lake City, it had extended to Ogden to connect with the Central Pacific-Southern Pacific (CP-SP), to Marysvale, Utah in the San Pedro Valley, to Heber, Utah and to Bingham and the Tintic Mining District. In those days of horse and buggy traveling, passenger trains were numerous and profitable.

In 1903 the Western Pacific, under consideration for a decade, was organized. By 1905 George Gould had to admit that he was the father. The planning and construction of the building was held up by the San Francisco earthquake in 1906 and a financial panic in 1907, but Gould was determined to build the line. The D&RG was put up as security for a bond issue to provide building funds. The WP was completed to Elko, Nevada in 1908 and to Salt Lake City in 1909. Limited operations began in August 1910.

THE BIRTH OF UNION STATION

The D&RG had 30 acres set aside for a depot in Salt Lake City as early as 1881. The first station that was built was a sprawling, two-story frame building suitable for a country town. Then, when building accelerated on the WP, a more grandiose station was planned to be ready in conjunction with the completion of the WP, and construction was begun. The new depot, formally called Union Station, was completed and opened in 1910, soon after the WP began operating.

The depot was overbuilt on a very elaborate and very large scale for two purposes. The first was to

Street side view of Salt Lake City Union Sation about 1910.
Utah Historical Society

demonstrate to the people of Salt Lake City and Utah that Gould, the WP and the D&RG expected the area to be a great and growing urban center. The second purpose of the overblown depot, of course, was to outdo the UP. It cost $750,000 and was designed by Henry S. Schlachs of Chicago.

The station is of no particular architectural style, but attempts to create an effect of richness and formality. It is two stories high, and the horizontal division of stories is emphasized by the use of different materials, colors and textures. There are many round arch windows. The focus is on the lower story. The upper one (that most people do not look at) was built of cheaper material. There is some surface ornamentation on the second story, however, including pilasters of square columns attached to the walls.

Union Station produced at least one unexpected result: Immigrants arriving in Salt Lake City tended to settle near it. A Greek community sprang up between 400 and 600 West; Italians settled near the depot; a Japanese community grew close by; and, Armenians settled west of the depot and tracks.

Edward H. Harriman of Kuhn, Loeb and Company consolidated ownership/control of the UP-CP-SP system at the end of March 1901. Eventually, the UP shut off the Ogden Gateway for CP-SP deliveries to the D&RG. In 1905—upon completion of the San Pedro, Los Angeles and Salt Lake City Railroad—it did the same at Salt Lake City.

The WP looked like a good way for the D&RG to counter the UP. It was used as a pawn in the fierce battle between Harriman and Gould. The D&RG was finally pauperized and sold at an auction for only $5 million. Arising from the ashes and reorganized as the Denver & Rio Grande Western, the "little road" dreamed of by William Jackson Palmer started its climb back up to become one of the great railroads of the West.

Loading Wool at Farmington on the Narrow Gauge

Moving the annual wool clip was always an event. When I was an agent at Pagosa Junction, Colorado, I was involved in the festivities by doing the paperwork for the Rio Grande.

The loading began at Farmington, New Mexico and moved east. Wool buyers from throughout the country and representatives from connecting railroads were on hand to influence the routing of traffic. Rio Grande traffic men were always on hand, plus two or three division officers. The one working railroad employee was an agent conscripted from the closest agency to make out the bills-of-lading and get contracts for the movement signed before returning to his agency to prepare waybills. The agent always missed the post-loading activities of eating and drinking sponsored by various traffic representatives.

Eventually, the Rio Grande studied what it cost to handle both the wool and livestock movements and found that it lost money on each car handled. Nor did those calculations include the salaries paid to traffic representatives or the money expended for influence: beds at the best hotels; high-proof liquid refreshments; the biggest, juiciest steaks with pie a la mode for dessert; and, cigars and brandy afterwards.

This picture was taken soon after completion of the Salt Lake City Union Station which served both the Rio Grande and Western Pacific. Note the trolley system poles. *Utah Historical Society*

The Rio Grande loaded wool in these large burlap bags; you can see the weight scales being used prior to loading. *Denver Public Library, Western History Section*

Romeo, Colorado

Romeo, Colorado, 21.56 miles south of Alamosa on the Cumbres Pass line of the Narrow Gauge, was the birthplace of Jack Dempsey and an early day sub-colony of the Salt Lake City Mormons. My first assignment as an agent-telegrapher for the Rio Grande was at Romeo, and my seniority date as a telegrapher started here on July 17, 1937.

Two days before I started at Romeo, I was in Denver finishing the geological report on the dam and canal sites of the Rio Grande Transmountain Bureau of Reclamation Project. With the completion of the report, I

Train #115 with Engine #475 is ready to depart Romeo, Colorado. *Denver Public Library, Western History Section*

The Big Hook at Green River, Utah on November 22, 1954.

This picture was taken the following day, Nov. 23, showing the large crane in operation lifting a derailed standard gauge box car. This accident resulted in quite a bit of twisted steel, as well as delayed train movements.

was laid off as field geologist and looking for a job. I called on J.W. Brunton, Rio Grande superintendent of communication and a good friend of my father. While I was talking with Brunton, he received a message that Ben Glaze, an agent at Romeo, was involved in an accident. Glaze stood on a bench that upended and caused him to break his foot. Glaze was on the way to the hospital, and the Romeo station was closed.

Brunton asked me if I knew how to telegraph. Without telling him how poor a Morse man I was, I told him I knew how. He never tested me, but told me to go to Romeo and start working. I did, and the Alamosa dispatchers demonstrated a lot of patience. About a year later, I took the Book of Rules examination. Later in the year, the Bureau of Reclamation recalled me, but I stayed with the Rio Grande. A budding geologist was lost to the fraternity.

Green River, Utah

Five days after I was transferred as trainmaster at Helper, Utah to trainmaster at Grand Junction, one of the biggest pileups took place on November 21, 1954 at Green River. The next week of my tenure as trainmaster west of Grand Junction was spent as senior officer clearing this wreck.

TOP. A flash flood came roaring down Saturnalia Gulch in 1921 and washed away most of the Rio Grande's yard tracks and just barely spared the main line. An eastbound freight train is able to proceed at reduced speed. J.B. Norwood, Sr. was night operator at Green River in 1920. Only a few months prior to the flood the Norwoods left and Norwood senior took employment with the RGS at Dolores, Colorado.

BOTTOM. We're looking southwest across the D&RGW tracks washed out by the 1921 flood. As a child, my favorite playground with my two sisters and other local youth was in this gulch hunting horned toads and lizards. *Both photos, Woolley, U.S. Geological Survey*

For about six months in 1920, our family lived at Green River, where my father worked as the second trick operator. At that time, Green River was a crew changing point. In 1919, headquarters for the newly formed Green River Division along with terminal facilities moved to Soldier Summit.

Across from the depot, numerous dugouts were built in the sandy hillside where crews lived in between assignments. Our abode was a weather-beaten, two-room shack set in a landscape of sand, tumbleweed and cactus. Our privy, like all others in the vicinity, consisted of four poles set in the ground with three burlap walls. The door was made from a wool sack suspended from the top frame with some rocks in the bottom to keep it from blowing open.

One morning just after sunup, we were disturbed by loud screams coming from one of these privies. Women, children and men carrying guns rushed to see

unsettled, untreated water direct from the river cost 25¢ per barrel; and, settled, chlorinated water cost 50¢ per barrel. A water wagon drawn by a team of horses made deliveries every other day.

The major crop at Green River was melons: cantaloupes, honeydews and watermelons that were grown along the river. The unused Rio Grande enginehouse was converted into a packing plant where the melons were packed, loaded and the bunkers of the cars were re-iced, if required. Pre-iced refrigerators arrived and were spotted, loaded and pulled. Ice was so precious that the children were never allowed to get close enough to the ice trains to steal any.

Transportation was a problem at Green River. When other areas with better transportation began raising plentiful crops, the melon business in Green River slumped. Around 1954, a strong, constant wind blew down the river during blossoming season and mixed pollen, including some from squash and pumpkin fields further up the river, with Green River's crop. The fine, sweet Green River strains of melons were contaminated, and the demand for them fell.

Cumbres

The population of Cumbres seldom reached as high as 20 people, even when the section men brought their children home during school vacations. The usual count was six or seven people, which included the operator, section foreman, car inspector and three or four section laborers. Unlike most stations along the line, there was never a crowd awaiting the daily arrival of the varnish.

This is not to imply that those stationed at the top of the Pass never listened for the sound of Train No. 215 whistling for Los Pinos or Train No. 216 whistling for Coxo (the first station in either direction of Cumbres). Unless occupied, each person made it a point to be on the platform when the train stopped. Seeing the same faces day after day and listening to the same voices recount the same stories became tiresome. The few minutes each day when the passenger trains stopped in town gave them relief from the monotony.

what was happening. When they got there, they found that one of their neighbors had taken her position on the throne and inadvertently disturbed migrating ants that were resting on the seat. The ants immediately mounted a defensive attack on her thighs.

A COSTLY DRINK

The Green River was a major water flow and close to town, but there were only a few wells, and these contained highly alkaline water. Water was precious:

We're overlooking the Los Pinos water tank on Cumbres Pass with locomotive #486 in the lead. The three carloads of lumber are followed by 10 tank cars of crude oil moved to Cumbres from Chama on the Chama-Cumbres Turn with two engines. A second turn of two engines brought up part of the box car loads. Then when the crews were rested, the #486 and helper brought the balance of the train up, and the three segments were consolidated at Cumbres for the #486 to bring them in. Photo was taken sometime in the early 1950s as the rear of the train consisted of pipe empties. *Dr. Richard Severance*

The perfumed breezes blowing from the spruce and balsam trees around the station created a very refreshing fragrance. The tall grass, especially after it rained, had its own aroma. Then there was a myriad of wild flowers including solid phalanxes of columbines, each emitting a distinctive fragrance that blended into one great, shattering essence. In late July, the crater lily blossoms were so perfumed that you could smell the fragrance all the way to the depot if the wind blew in the right direction.

Cumbres was a fine place to be assigned in the summer. Unfortunately, the only time I was ever assigned there was in the middle of winter. I and the section men drank a lot of coffee and waited for the train's whistle.

Poncha Junction

I was working as night operator at Chama, New Mexico in 1938, and at that time, the job only paid $125 per month (less a 90¢ deduction for hospitalization). Our rent was $12 per month, and I scrounged coal for fuel at our coal chute. In spite of this, we had a debt of $150 at the grocery store with little hope of reducing it regardless of how miserly we were.

A temporary job was advertised at Poncha Junction for a 90-day period during the stock rush. This job was added in order to facilitate train movements, which were difficult to dispatch due to erratic and unpredictable trains running to and from the Monarch Branch. In addition to the regular daytime shift, the Poncha Junction operator averaged two or three calls a night. For each call, he received three hours pay, even though he might be on duty for only 10 minutes. During the 90 days I worked at Poncha Junction, my monthly wages were between $300 and $400.

The Rio Grande furnished kerosene for lights (lamps) and coal for fuel. In the back of the station/ living quarters, there was a clear, non-freezing stream choked with watercress where we got our water supply, also free. At Salida, the Safeway store was trying to throttle competition by almost giving away groceries. By the end of the first month, we had some extra money, and our grocery bill at the Chama Mercantile was marked "Paid."

WINDS BLOW COLD AND WARM

It was not all beer and skittles. The living quarters behind the office had rough, pine floors that were cracked and less than level. The window frames were loose, and there were a few broken panes. The wind never stopped blowing, and a metal extension on the chimney, which was necessary to get a good draft, kept blowing off. This chimney was attached to the kitchen stove, which was the only heating source for the big living room. The warmth generated by the cast-iron heater in the office contributed little to the heat from the kitchen stove.

The plumbing consisted of a large galvanized bath tub that we bought with our newly acquired wealth and for which we used to carry water from the creek to heat on the range. Even then, bathing was not comfortable because cold air blew through the floor, walls and windows.

The second plumbing item was an outdoor privy. Over the years, the rear of the privy had sunk about a foot, so when you sat on the throne, your bottom was at an acute angle. The seat was like sitting on a block of ice until I covered it with some scraps of shaggy carpeting.

A requirement of the job was for the incumbent to be available 24 hours per day, seven days a week (unless the dispatcher granted permission to be absent for a few hours). Consequently, there was no enter-

The Poncha Junction station and living quarters were fairly simple. Not much luxury, but the scenery made up for it. The Monarch Branch was straight ahead up the track. *M.D. McCarter collection*

TOP. Another view of Poncha Junction station. BELOW. Engine #480 leaves Poncha Junction with empties for the Monarch Branch quarry in the spring of 1950. *Both photos M.D. McCarter collection*

tainment, although we did buy a small battery-operated radio.

Each Sunday, we exchanged dinners with the section foreman Joe Ventura, his lovely wife, Julia, and their daughters. Besides her Italian grace and good looks, Julia was also a superb cook of Italian cuisine. Joe maintained a large supply of red wines of the "primo," first-run quality. We had the best of both worlds alternating between Italian cooking one Sunday and southern states American cooking the next.

REQUIRED ASSISTANCE

The road between the station and the Ventura's sectionhouse was only native soil. When the snows came, the road turned to mud in the daytime, and the ruts froze at night. Quite frequently when returning home from the Ventura's, I required assistance from my wife to keep from falling on the rough roadbed. I also needed assurance that the ruts were not as wide and deep as the Grand Canyon, which after an evening of drinking Joe's wines, is often the way those ruts appeared to me.

I never returned to my regular/permanent assignment at Chama. The Crested Butte agency came up for bid, and I was senior bidder.

So, when Poncha Junction closed for the season, I

climbed the semaphore mast and removed the blades. We bought a hugh supply of the bargain-priced groceries at Salida to take with us, loaded what little furniture we owned into a box car, and headed for Crested Butte.

We did not owe anyone. We had nearly $500 in surplus cash, and a resolve to never again buy on credit.

Crested Butte

Crested Butte in the summer of 1939 did not look much different than it did when this picture was taken in 1930. However, we did not first approach it during summer. The temporary job at Poncha Junction was finished just before Christmas 1938, when snow depth in the Monarch Quarry closed it down for that season.

The road in the left foreground was paved sometime after 1930, and we were driving on pavement as we approached the point where the picture was taken. At least there was a paved road under the icy, snow-packed trough that meandered between two walls of drifted snow. We could not see the town because of a

The agent lived upstairs at Crested Butte in this rather regal depot; at one time the bay window had a train order board over it, at least until the Floresta Branch closed. *Colorado Historical Society*

Crested Butte about 1930 looked like this from a distance. *Photo courtesy Bernice Gardiner, Jamy B. Day collection*

heavy, wind-driven snow storm. All we could see was that we were nearing the end of a nerve-wracking trip, having driven through blizzard conditions all the way from Poncha Junction over Monarch Pass to Gunnison and on to Crested Butte.

We spent the night in the Colorado Fuel & Iron Company miner's hotel, ate a meal of heavy Polish cooking and did not get any sleep. The steam radiators could not be shut off, and the CF&I did not ration coal to feed the furnance. The radiator in our room was so hot that a pair of cherished nylon hose my wife thoughtlessly laid across the radiator dissolved into a blob of synthetics.

Our household goods arrived, so early the next day, I drafted the section gang and car inspector to help move us into the agent's quarters over the office of the depot.

The quarters had not been used for some time. They contained cobwebs and were dirty with several boxes of miscellaneous items of a previous agent named Mickey Boyle. Later, in going through the old boxes, I found a large envelope of Boyle's personal records. He was a devout Catholic and was either a great sinner or made provision for sinning. There were dispensations from the Catholic Church for violating all of the 10 Commandments except "Thou Shalt Not Kill." He even had one, dealing with adultery, that cost him a pretty penny.

TRYING TO KEEP WARM

The first order of the day was the installation of stoves. Immediately after setting them up, we started

fires in them. The fires were just going good when smoke began pouring from both stoves. Dousing the fires, I pulled the flues to inspect the chimney that served both stoves. Four or five bricks had tumbled from the crown and lodged at the flue openings. These were removed, the flues replaced, and we soon began to have heat.

Later that winter, we had one more mess involving our heating system. The office was heated by an enormous cast iron roundhouse stove that stood in the center of the office. About 10 feet of flue was suspended by wires and ran to the chimney that served this stove. A two-foot-square register was cut into the ceiling in order to allow heat to rise to the living quarters. The CF&I coal used for fuel made a lot of soot, and the pipe had not been cleaned on a regular basis. When it finally exploded, it blew soot all over the office and up through the register into our living quarters. What a mess! My wife scrubbed and cleaned for a week, and I never did get everything in the office cleaned.

AN IDYLLIC LIFE

There was no indoor plumbing at Crested Butte. By the coming of spring, we walked a path to the privy between walls of snow. The station cistern, containing water usually hauled from Gunnison, froze solid, and I had to carry water from a deep well about a block away. Washing days required many trips, and bath nights were almost as bad.

Aside from winter, life at Crested Butte among first and second generation mining people, with its excel-

32

lent hunting and even better fishing, was idyllic. Next to Chama, it was the favorite of all the stations I worked while still on line.

We made a number of close friends there. The Gilberts and Tulleys were our outdoor buddies, and we spent almost every Saturday and Sunday during the summer and fall fishing or hunting. During the winter, we spent many evenings playing cards with Joe Moraskey and his wife, Carmin.

The altitude was too high for my wife; she was pregnant, so climbing the stairs to our quarters became impractical. She went to Chama awaiting confinement. I stayed at Crested Butte until April, then traded my agency for a night telegraph job at Antonito, Colorado.

You would not recognize Crested Butte today. The big mine shut down nearly four decades ago, the population mix changed, and the advent of winter sport facilities and condominiums has served to create a more prosperous community, but to my way of thinking, one that is less ideal.

Denver Union Station

Before the year 1880 passed into history, a number of large and costly Denver buildings were to be constructed in the following spring. They were: the Tabor Opera House, the Windsor Hotel, the Tabor Block (all H.A.W. Tabor enterprises), City Hall, the Court House, the Cathedral, Barclay Block, and Union Depot.

The Union Depot was slated to be the finest railway structure west of Chicago. Funds to build it came from a stock company capitalized at $400,000. The company consisted of the different railroads which were to use the depot. At this time, the company owned only 12 acres of ground, but later acquired more.

The architecture of the depot was Modern Gothic. The building was on the east side of the Platte River at the foot of 16th, 17th and 18th streets. Later additions carried to 15th Street. Original dimensions were 503 feet long and 65 feet wide. In years to come, addition after addition changed these dimensions greatly. At the southeast corner stood a tower 165 feet high that served no useful purpose. It was built of volcanic tuff from the Castle Rock, Colorado quarries located approximately 30 miles south of Denver on the D&RG Railroad; trimming stone came from quarries at Morrison and Manitou, Colorado.

The first floor of the depot was devoted to passenger service, express service and mail. The second floor contained offices for the staffs of railroads using the facility. For the period, the depot was exemplary. It was well ventilated, heated by steam, and even was

THE BUSIEST PLACE IN DENVER

Denver Union Depot never achieved its goal as the finest railroad structure west of Chicago, but for the West, it was an impressive accomplishment and a vitally needed and much used facility. Hundreds of thousands of new arrivals passed through it to man the many developing mines, pineries, industries and livestock ranges. Recruits off to three wars said goodbye to families and friends; those who returned received their welcome home in the great high-ceiling concourse.

Up to and even during the Great Depression, the depot was the busiest place in Denver. The period that may most reasonably be called its "good old days" extended between about 1888 and 1893. Silver was king, coal was queen, and the timberlands were being worked to build facilities and homes for the kingdom. Cattle and sheep grazed on the lush pastures of the highlands and produce was flowing from the virgin soil to feed the people of the realm.

These hordes of people coming to the "promised land" came from all over the world. They came from the Balkans, the middle of Europe, the Latin countries, the Dark Continent and Asia. A foreigner anxious to hear the language of his homeland did not have to search long. Within the waiting room of Denver Union Station, it was like a modern day Tower of Babel—the sound of America in the making.

THE DECLINE

In the decade of 1930-1940, I was infrequently part of the depot's crowd. The following decade I hardly saw it at all, but from 1950 until my retirement in 1975, I saw a lot of it. So I lived with it during some 15 years of relative activity and use, and suffered with it during its decline and virtual demise.

World War II and its aftermath killed Denver Union Depot and similar facilities all over the country. They were designed to handle railroad passenger trains and passengers who were willing to move at a slow pace. More to the point, the passengers had very little choice in the matter. Highways were not numerous or well-maintained; automobiles were not yet plentiful or affordable; and, airplanes awaited the ultimate development of World War II. If people wanted or needed to travel, they traveled by train.

People seldom perceive, or admit to, an impending debacle, and therefore, leave no records of what was happening. This is all too true with the Denver Union Station. One railroad after another ceased to operate, was absorbed by another, or reduced service as demand decreased. This picture of Union Station's future was clear, but no one paid heed.

Wartime needs for large earth-moving equipment were fulfilled. Transport on the battlefields birthed powerful trucks and automobiles. Giant, dependable pilots were trained to fly them.

The war over, plants converted to models suitable for civilian use. Miles of highways, including freeways, were built. Airports increased prolifically. Motels appeared along highways. Americans wanted to travel fast in their own automobiles—to stop at night where they wanted. Or better yet, they could fly.

Passenger trains and union stations, including the one at Denver, were doomed. The imposing stone Gothic building broods at the foot of 16th Street and dreams of the good old days. The Tower of Babel is silent; only a few people come or go with the once a day Amtrak train.

The years 1888-1893 unquestionably were the "good old days" of the Denver Union Station. No one is left to tell us what it was like back then. We have only the tales passed down from them to the following generations. A few old photos, yellowed news clippings and travel books, along with overstated claims in advertisements issued by the railroads of Colorado, give us some idea about the past.

If nostalgia strikes, read everything you can find, look at old photos and listen to the stories passed down. Go to the depot to sit on one of the old waiting room benches and dream with the old building. Shut your eyes, open your ears and try to relive a day here in 1890.

A DAY IN THE LIFE OF UNION DEPOT

The day begins with the noise and confusion of switch engines placing outbound morning trains on the proper tracks and pulling overnight inbound trains to the various railroads' passenger yards. There, they will be readied for their next assignment. Hostlers add to the confusion, trying to put engines on trains that are to leave and cutting off engines to take to their roundhouses. Despite the efforts of the hostlers and switch engine firemen, each engine is adding dark sulfurous smoke to the murk already under the sheds left over from the preceding evening.

Every engine has a bell ringing to warn the army of mail, baggage and express handlers, engaged in moving the almost unwieldy carts and wagons to or from trains, to load or unload as needed. It is so murky from smoke that hand signals cannot be seen. Lantern signals, not much brighter than fireflies, flicker all over the place. The first rays of the rising sun do nothing to brighten the situation. Reference to the Tower of Babel applies to the waiting room; here it is Dantean.

Conductors from the railroads and their brakemen come from the locker rooms enroute to their trains. Regardless of which road they travel, they are uniformly dressed in suits of a dark blue material; the coats are buttoned by large shiny brass buttons. On their heads are flat-topped caps with patent leather visors bearing a brass badge that reads either "Conductor" or "Brakeman." Each carries the universal keister, a leather bag like a Gladstone. In addition, the brakemen carry their flagging kits.

Pullman conductors and porters, dressed almost identically, follow them out to the trains. Enginemen stop below the large standard clock located above the exit, check their watches and register the fact in books of various railroads lying on a tall table near the exit.

On the interior wall to the left of the clock is a plaque dedicated to William Jackson Palmer, "Union Cavalry General—Pioneer—Railroad Builder."

On the waiting room benches are weary women and their broods. They have slept and rested there while awaiting a train that will carry them toward waiting husbands and fathers. Now, rays from the rising sun struggle diligently to pierce the grime of the windows high above the first floor. The few that are successful are eliminated before they reach the waiting room floor. They die among the tendrils of engine, cigar and pipe smoke that constantly hangs in the dome.

Passengers who can afford it go to the coffee shop and restaurant. The majority open baskets and bags to breakfast on sausages, cheese and black bread. After the ship and train fares from the continent, there is little left for the luxury of restaurant fare.

The fully risen sun greets a line of pedestrians and vehicles coming down 16th Street toward the depot—passengers for the day's train. As they arrive, they enter the portals to promptly queue-up at the long line of ticket windows. A haughty dowager tries to muscle in line ahead of a red-haired Irish girl. She is forcefully shoved to one side and admonished in strident Irish brogue: "Come on, sister! Get back where you belongs."

A scrawny dog slips in between the legs of arriving passengers to scrounge bits of lunch scraps. He is challenged by one of the fat, pampered cats tolerated around the station for their talent at killing rats and mice. A snarling, spitting fight breaks out. Children cheer. Women scream and clamber up on benches. Station policemen arrive and swing batons to quell the battle. The dog flees out the door yelping, and the cat ambles arrogantly away with its tail sticking straight up, bushy and ready for more trouble.

There was no formal segregation in the Denver Union Station waiting room, but people did tend to gather by nationalities, profession or color. That is, until the ticket lines began to form. Then, it was every man and woman for himself/herself, first come, first served, and the devil take the hindmost. If you did not obtain a ticket in time to catch your train, you waited for the next one. Death, taxes and 1890 passenger trains waited for no one.

While the cat and dog fight is in progress, pickpockets plied their trade. When it is over the panhandlers resume their plea of "Brother, can you spare a dime?" Over in the corner an inebriated cowboy takes the last

Denver Union Station in early 1900. *W.H. Jackson, Colorado Historical Society*

The Denver Union Station in the 1970s and in the days of Amtrak; the horses are gone, the people are gone, the Mizpah arch is gone. *M.D. McCarter collection*

drink from his bottle and flings it to break against a wall. Seconds later, he is reeling from the blow of a station cop's truncheon and headed to the paddy wagon.

A well-fed, derbied drummer walks into the barbershop for his morning shave. Leaving, he jingles four or five brass checks in his hand. They are of brass, two inches in diameter, and around the perimeter is embossed "Silver Dollar Hotel Denver, Colo." In the center of the circle of letters is the statement, "Good For One Screw, Ruth Campbell, Prop." These brass checks were sold by all shoeshine boys, barbers and cab drivers. They paid $9 for 10 and sold them for $1 each.

THE SHOW TO COME

For the men in the waiting room, the event of the day is about to happen. A macquereaux enters the portal followed by two of his fillies. Well-dressed in a dove-gray suit and a silk top hat, he cannot compete with the two Circuit Riding Cyprians he escorts. Brightly, but not gaudily dressed, with a touch of makeup on their faces, they gracefully walk to a bench in their high-top buttoned shoes. Just a bit of their silk-stockinged ankles show, and all male eyes look at them. Their "manager" stands nearby twirling his gold-headed Malacca cane.

A genteel lady, who was occupying the same bench, arises in a huff, gathers her belongings and moves to another bench. The group awaits an announcement of their train, although how anyone could distinguish what the train announcer is saying in his constant litany is a mystery.

These peripatetic prostitutes are enroute to Glenwood Springs, Aspen, Leadville, Salida, Cripple Creek, Trinidad, Walsenburg, Durango, Silverton and Rico. From assignment to assignment, they travel a circuit made easy by the trains going anywhere where there are lonesome men with money. They are not crib girls, but the créme de la créme of their profession.

That grand old Gothic piece of architecture, the Denver Union Station, remembers many such mornings and evenings. World War II brought automobiles, interstate highways, government-subsidized airports and 747 airplanes, motels—and people in a hurry. The arrival and departure of the daily Amtraks with their few passengers and the weekend ski trains run in winter cause this "old girl" to weep as she remembers the good old days.

The Ghost Terminal

At the crest of Soldier Summit, Utah, about one mile west of Highway 50 and a little west of an unimproved road Soldier Summit to Duchesne, Utah, are the almost forgotten graves of some soldiers who were killed in one of the skirmishes of Utah's last Indian War, the Blackhawk War, 1865-1868, against the Ute Indians. The rains, snow falls and winds blow over the skeletons in the graves of this 7,400 foot pass.

The same rains, snow falls and winds blow where a once major terminal of the Denver and Rio Grande, later the Denver & Rio Grande Western Railroad, was active. Associated with this now ghost terminal are also skeletons of venality, mistakes in judgement, lack of common railroad sense and misused money. The terminal has been gone 68 years, and the area it once covered is as bare of remains as the soldiers' graves; all traces were removed or reclaimed by the environment.

U.S. RAILROAD ADMINISTRATION

World War I erupted in Europe in July 1914. Regardless of Woodrow Wilson's predictions and statements, it was apparent by 1915 that the United States would be drawn into the conflict.

It was also readily apparent that the U.S. was woefully unprepared to wage war. Of major concern was the deteriorated condition of all the railroads that were to bear the burden of land transportation. No one was exempt; the D&RG was in as poor condition as any.

In 1916, the U.S. Congress passed the National Defense Act, and in August of that year, the Council of National Defense became active. The U.S. entered the war on April 6, 1917, and, by December, the railroads were hard-pressed financially and unable to keep up with the demands for transportation.

In 1918, the U.S. Railroad Administration was founded, and the government took over operation of the railroads. This lasted for 26 months, until March 1920. Opportunists rushed to become part of this effort to keep the railroads. As in any war, accountability for performance or expenditures of money was ignored.

The U.S. Railroad Administration, which, under impossible conditions, assumed responsibility in a time of national crisis; however, it must be admitted that there were countless incidents of poor judgement, decisions and plans perpetrated by administrators with little or no knowledge or experience of railroads. A great deal of money was wasted on impractical hare-brained ideas as well as monies that simply disappeared and were never accounted for. The building of the Soldier Summit mountain top terminal was a flagrant example of this type of waste.

THE D&RG

The financial and physical situation of the D&RG (it

Moving the earth and rebuilding terrain where the terminal at Soldier Summit will be built. The date is about 1918. *Colorado Historical Society*

The Soldier Summit square enginehouse and incline to the coal dump used to fuel locomotives. Water for the engines had to be pumped in from miles away; snow was a big problem as note the snow fences off to the right behind the coal dump. A few years later this whole complex was closed and moved to Helper. *Colorado Historical Society*

became the Denver & Rio Grande Western on July 31, 1921) must be understood to fully appreciate the foolishness of building a terminal at Soldier Summit.

The Missouri Pacific and Jay Gould held controlling interest in the D&RG when financing of the Western Pacific was needed. They put up the D&RG as security for $5 million worth of bonds. The D&RG, in acquiescing to this arrangement, thought it was only guaranteeing payment of interest on the bonds. Later, after many lawsuits, the courts interpreted provisions of controlling agreements otherwise, ruling that the D&RG was also responsible for the bonds.

In 1916, the Western Pacific was foreclosed. Bondholders quickly requested the D&RG to make good on the bonds. In January 1917, $3 million of D&RG cash was impounded. In August, the bondholders were awarded $38 million payable by the D&RG. On January 3, 1918, the judgement was upheld. As a possession of the D&RG, the Utah Fuel Company went on the block and was sold for $4 million.

Gould was milking the D&RG for years, and no money was spent on maintenance. By the time the war clouds were gathering, the plant and equipment of the D&RG were rapidly approaching obsolescence.

There was no way the judgement in favor of the bondholders could be satisfied.

With the assumption of operations by the government and guaranteed payment of costs, plus a grant of $3 million by the government to make the most urgently needed repairs, the D&RG could breathe a little easier. In May 1918, the Railroad Administration set a fixed sum of $8,319,000 as guaranteed compensation to the D&RG in order to make up any amount short of penalty.

DANGEROUS AND RAPIDLY GROWING WORSE

The Esch-Cummins Bill returned operations and control of the railroads to their owners efective March 1, 1920. The D&RG, physically and financially, was but slightly better off than it was in 1916. Its physical condition continued to deteriorate to a degree that it gained the sobriquet "Dangerous and Rapidly Growing Worse" about 1923 when its condition was at its worse.

Six months after the Railroad Administration returned the railroad to the owners, the D&RG was put on the auction block. This happened on September 25, 1920. On November 20, 1920, the railroad was sold for $5 million; $86 million of common and preferred stock was wiped out. A new railroad company, the Denver & Rio Grande Western Railroad Company, incorporated under Delaware laws came into existence on July 31, 1921. It was cleared of indebtedness connected with the old company, but still in dire straits. The Salt Lake City shops were practically shut down; the major shops at Burnham (Denver) were hardly in better shape. Track gangs were reduced to doing hardly more than tightening anglebar bolts and resetting spikes.

Somewhere along the way, the $3 million grant and the $8.3 million guarantee were spent, and still, the railroad was hardly operable. However, up on top of Soldier Summit there was an albatross of a terminal that cost some $5 million to put into operation. The same amount of money would have put the railroad in an enviable condition if it was spent more wisely. Construction costs were the least costly items. Train and terminal operating costs were greater and never improved.

THE FIASCO

Robert G. Athearn in his definitive book *Rebel of the Rockies* mentions Soldier Summit only two times, both briefly. One mentions a line change made in 1913 at a cost of $2.5 million that lengthened the line over Soldier Summit, but reduced the grade from 4 percent to 2 percent. The other is captioned with a picture of the terminal taken in the 1920s. The caption states that from November 1919 until November 1929, this terminal was in operation. Light engines were run down hill to Helper, on the east, and down to Thistle, on the west, to assist trains.

The concept of having a major terminal at the summit of a mountain, specifically Soldier Summit, was neither feasible nor practical for a number of reasons:

- In territory requiring helper engines, it is better to put the helper on at the foot of the grade, newly and completely serviced and supplied, thereby eliminating delays.
- At Soldier Summit, fuel for engines was hauled uphill 25 miles and raised 1,610 feet. In winter this coal, loaded in open-topped cars, was often frozen and difficult to dump.
- Sufficient water for railroad and community use was pumped a little over two miles.
- In winter, strong, cold winds blew, and snow fell heavily and piled in deep drifts. During, and for a period after a snowstorm, a large section gang had to work around the clock clearing switches and facilities, in some instances removing packed, drifted snow from around cars on the yard tracks.
- Under winter conditions, switchmen and other forces were handicapped trying to move while heavily dressed.

Finally in 1929, the D&RGW made a sensible decision by establishing a sub-terminal at Thistle to care for the Marysvale Branch and helper engines for eastbound trains over Soldier Summit. On the other side of the mountain, a terminal was established at Helper, Utah. Two good marshalling yards, and adequate engine and car facilities were provided, and westbound helper engines were placed in trains here. All of the faults at Soldier Summit, and others not mentioned here, were eliminated or minimized by moving the terminal off the top of the mountain. This ridiculous experiment conceived and born under stress of war times ended.

Soldier Summit's railroad company-owned hotel, dwellings and operating headquarters built to care for workers by the Rio Grande. Note that the equipment had not yet been re-stenciled to "Denver & Rio Grande Western."

The terminal at Soldier Summit, Utah opened in 1919 at a cost of $1.25 million to expedite the Carbon County coal movement. The idea was not successful. *Colorado Historical Society*

Form 3530—12-13-300M

DENVER AND RIO GRANDE RAILROAD
OIL TICKET

Date _Aug 15 1914_

Station _Durango_

Engine No. _6_

From _Dgo_ to _Rico_

Valve Oil	_3_	pts.
Car Oil	_5_	pts.
Rod Cup Grease		lbs.
Driving Box Grease		lbs.
Wool Packing		lbs.
Headlight Oil		pts.
Signal Oil		pts.
Cotton Waste	_1_	lbs.
Wool Waste		lbs.

_____
Roundhouse Foreman

DENVER & RIO GRANDE SYSTEM.
COAL TICKET.

Date _7 3_ 190_7_

Station _Dgo_

_15 202_ **3 Ton**

Eng. No. _____ Engr. _McDonold_

Car No. _9423_ Initial _Dgs_ Pocket _____

Engine #489 in May of 1955 on Marshall Pass with a trainload of rail from abandonment. *Dr. Richard Severence*

Chapter 3

Famous Locations on the D&RG

Discovering Marshall Pass

Two government surveys worked in the Colorado Rocky Mountains in 1873. One was led by F.V. Hayden, and the other was led by Lieutenant Wheeler, who worked in the San Juan area. Wheeler's party included Lieutenant William L. Marshall, for whom Marshall Pass was named.

Marshall developed a toothache near Silverton and traveled to Denver for medical treatment. Marshall and

a packer named Dave Mears (no relation to Otto Mears) left the party at Silverton and traveled through Cimarron Pass to Lake City, Colorado. They proceeded to the location where Sargents, Colorado later developed. From there, they followed a creek, which now is named Marshall Creek, and then ascended the range to a saddle that was later to be named Marshall Pass Summit and where the Denver & Rio Grande

A one-car inspection party looks at newly-built track probably around Marshall Pass. D&RG No. 1 the *Montezuma* has no air compressor. *W.H. Jackson, Colorado Historical Society*

station was located. No one knows whether they descended down Grays Creek or Shirley Creek, but they journeyed to the point where the two junctioned and formed Poncha Creek. They continued to Salida, and from there, they proceeded to Denver.

Marshall recorded and reported his route over the pass to his Army superiors, inferring that it was a new pass over the range. As a result, U.S. Army cartographers named it Marshall Pass. The credit given Marshall was an error. The route Marshall and Dave Mears traveled was used for many years by indians, trappers, traders and Otto Mears.

MEARS' TOLL ROAD

Otto Mears built a toll road over Poncha Pass from Saguache, Colorado to Salida. Next, he built a toll road up Poncha Creek to the junction of Grays Creek and Shirley Creek, and, from there, he built over the most advantageous terrain to the summit of Marshall Pass and descended to Tomichi Creek. Except for a few changes in the route to make a better road for wagons, Mears followed the old trail. William Jackson Palmer of the Denver & Rio Grande paid Mears $13,000 for the rights to the road and, when built, the D&RG very closely approximated Mears' road.

The elevation at Salida is 7,050 feet; at Marshall Pass, it is 10,846 feet. The distance from Salida to

It's a sad day as #489 and a long string of gondolas and a crane pick up rail from the west end of Gunnison Yard in Colorado during May of 1955. The final days of the Narrow Gauge in its original state were nearly over. *Dr. Richard Severence*

W.H. Jackson took this classic picture of the east side of Marshall Pass from Mears Junction to the summit, and caught three—count'em—three trains going west at the same time! A similar photo without the trains appears in *Rio Grande Narrow Gauge Recollections. Colorado Historical Society*

Marshall Pass is 26 miles, and the railroad climbs 3,796 feet between these two points. From Mears Junction to Marshall Pass, the governing grade is 4 percent with a maximum curvature of 24 degrees.

OTHER DISTINCTIONS

Marshall Pass has one other distinction. In 1880, riding in one of the Sanderson & Barlow stages that regularly used Mears' toll road, former President General Ulysses S. Grant traveled over Marshall Pass to inspect the mining operations in the Pitkin area. He probably had other motives than just sightseeing because during this period, General Grant was involved in Union Pacific Railroad matters. The Union Pacific, for all practical purposes, owned the often-renamed Denver, South Park & Pacific Railroad. The Union Pacific desperately wanted a route over the mountains to the developing mines, livestock and timber in the Gunnison area, so Grant possibly was scouting for this route.

JACKSON'S WORK

Pictures of the east side of Marshall Pass in later years were often taken from the same location as in Jackson's photographs. Admittedly, there were advantages in being the official photographer of the D&RG. It was not unusual for Jackson to select the location for a picture and then enhance the setting by having the D&RG set up train movements and locations as he desired. This may very well be such a picture because the three trains are located at perfect positions in this scene. Notice that the trains are all smoking, a prerequisite for all railroad action shots to this day.

The canvas tents and the wooden shack construction camp of Shirley at Milepost 229 was in the meadow at the left center of the photo. Upon arrival of tracks at Sargents, Colorado (the bottom of Marshall Pass on the west side), Shirley immediately was abandoned, leaving no trace of the camp. The D&RG reached Gunnison, Colorado on August 6, 1881. Jackson's picture was probably made the following year.

There was another, more substantial camp at Mears Junction at Milepost 226 that was involved in building over Poncha Pass. A side track named Keene was located between Shirley and Grays. Grays was at Milepost 234 at the head of Grays Creek; Marshall Pass was at Milepost 241.

In the days of the small engine, there were water tanks at Mears, Shirley, Grays and Marshall Pass. With the emergence of the K-Class engines, not all of the water tanks were needed at these locations. So, the tanks at Shirley and Grays were dismantled.

SNOW ON MARSHALL PASS

Marshall Pass did not receive as much snow as Cumbres Pass, but at the summit, the winds were much

The snowsheds were only partially completed when this photo was taken at Marshall Pass. The tower at the east end of the shed was for the gratification of passengers and excursionists to view the area. *W.H. Jackson, Colorado Historical Society*

stronger and more constant. What snow did fall tended to drift badly.

Construction went ahead during the winter of 1880-1881 under miserable conditions. When the rails reached the summit, one of the first trains run was loaded with timber and lumber to build snowsheds. Carpenters accompanied the supplies and quickly went to work building the sheds. It seemed like there were never enough sheds. Up until final abandonment, additions and improvements were in progress. All living quarters for employees stationed at Marshall Pass were under cover of the sheds. There was a covered wye as well.

The sheds were so extensive that it was necessary to build ventilation and smoke vents above the roofs at the expected depths of the snow. Fans were never installed, and, while engines were under the shed or moving through it, the shed filled completely with smoke.

From the beginning, summer excursions from Salida were popular. As an added attraction, a tower was built just outside the west end of the sheds. Looking west from this tower, vistas of spruce surrounding alpine meadows of lush grass and brilliant flowers covered the landscape. In the other direction, there were

high, rugged peaks capped with snow. Towards the north was Mount Ouray (elevation, 14,043 feet); beyond it was Mount Antero (elevation, 14,245 feet); Mount Harvard (elevation, 14,375 feet); and Mount Shavano (elevation, 14,239 feet). Flatlanders were always mesmerized by this view.

Dotsero Cutoff

The first application for authority to build the Dotsero Cutoff was made on December 12, 1928. After much haggling, litigation and searching for funds, the Reconstruction Finance Committee (RFC) granted a loan of $3,850,000 on September 12, 1932. Within two weeks, construction began with a target completion date of September 15, 1934.

The dedication ceremony took place on June 16, 1934. More litigation and searching for funds followed. Most of the financial help was from the RFC, and, as a result, that portion of the Denver & Salt Lake/Denver & Rio Grande Western between Denver and Dotsero was operated by the RFC. It was not until June 1946 that unrestricted operation was possible. At this time uncontested authority was granted in

The D&RG ran a scenic excursion to Marshall Pass on August 29, 1883, and these are the people who went. Shed construction was still in progress at right. *W.H. Jackson, Colorado Historical Society*

Locomotive #472 is on the point of a six-car *Shavano* passenger train downgrade west of Marshall Pass. *Colorado Historical Society*

#3600 was on hand for the Dotsero dedication ceremonies June 16, 1934. Denver Public Library, Western History Section

Aerial view of Dotsero cut-off dedication shows all the activities; hundreds showed up for the event. Craig Branch line diverges off to the right and along the hillside in the picture. *Denver Public Library, Western History Section*

order for the D&SL and D&RGW to consolidate. The D&RGW came out of receivership on April 11, 1947.

There is a mistaken belief that the station at Dotsero was named Dotsero for surveying purposes because it was station zero between Denver-Pueblo and Ogden. This is not true. The junction point near Bond, where the D&SL tracks to Craig were established upon completion of the Cutoff, was named Orestod, which is Dotsero spelled backwards.

In the 1923 roster, Dotsero is shown as Milepost 342.66 from Denver with a track capacity of 18 cars. Dotsero is also named in a 1909 newspaper account describing a head-on collision of D&RGW trains in which 23 people were killed. The engineman misread his watch and passed Dotsero on the other train's time. Siloam Springs at Milepost 344.52 was the next station. It no longer exists.

Phantom Curve

Between Antonito and Cumbres, Colorado, between Toltec Siding and the location of the old Toltec sectionhouse, at about Milepost 307.5, there is a tall spire of light-colored andesite. This spire is the midpoint of a curve. Approached from either the east or west at night, in the headlight beams of a locomotive or the rays of the moon, this formation looks like a specter or phantom. Hence, the curve is called Phantom Curve.

One of the many Colorado-New Mexico state line crossings is on the middle of a high fill just west of the Phantom at Milepost 307.30. When the line was first pushed toward the San Juan country, this drainage was crossed on a timber bridge. Fill eventually replaced the bridge, but it never lost the appellation Phantom Curve.

Two accidents occurred on Phantom Curve. The first resulted in fatalities, and the second caused minor injuries.

W.H. Jackson's picture of Phantom Curve depicts members of an excursion train who have walked ahead to do some sightseeing while the train waits for the signal to pick them up. This picture was probably taken in the early 1880s, judging by the ladies' dress and by the fact that the bridge west of the curve is filled. This was done a few years after the fatal wreck that occurred soon after the D&RG reached Durango on July 27, 1881.

A Durango newspaper reported the accident as being 32 miles west of Antonito and two miles west of Toltec Tunnel No. 1 (today, the Mud Tunnel). This placed the wreck on the bridge west of the Phantom.

The newspaper writer for the *Durango Miner* went into all the gory details of the wreck, but failed to give any date of the accident. By inference, the year was either 1882 or 1883. The newsclip was not dated

either. The writer states that "from week to week since the first of March, the *Miner* has continued to warn the public of the unsafe condition of the San Juan extension of the D. & R.G. Railroad." So, the railroad had operated at least one year prior to this wreck.

Eliminating most of the hyperbole, the accident described a westbound train consisting of an engine, a passenger car and a caboose that originated at Alamosa. There were 15 men and one woman in the coach, and six men, presumably railroad workers, in the caboose. At a point that calculations reveal to be on the approach of the bridge just west of Phantom Curve, while moving at an estimated speed of 15 mph, the coach derailed and bumped over the ties for a short distance. The car first leaned toward the mountain, then changed the direction of its tilt and turned over. The car rolled over four times and came to rest in a splintered condition some 50 feet below the track level. The writer also states the car rolled 200 feet from the rails before it stopped. This is only one of his inconsistencies.

Nothing indicated that the caboose overturned. The engine did not because it was run on to Osier to inform authorities and ask for help. It then returned to the accident with section men and a flatcar. The eight injured people were taken to Osier on this car, but only three survived. The woman was among the dead.

A relief train arrived and took the dead and injured to Antonito. Apparently, the track at the wreckage site was still passable because a special train left Antonito and took everyone to Alamosa.

SECOND WRECK

The second memorable wreck at Phantom Curve was on February 11, 1948 when the eastbound *San Juan* was struck by a snowslide near the location where the excursionists are standing in the photograph. Striking the two rear cars with terrific force, the avalanche shoved them over the side of the roadbed. The parlor/lounge car hung up on the rock where the telegraph pole is seen in the photograph. The other car rode the slide and stopped another 100 feet down the mountainside.

The brakeman, Sid Skirvin, sustained cracked ribs when an aspen tree speared the coach and grazed his body. Conductor Ed Morgan had a portion of his scalp torn away from the bone, but it was sewn back. He had no recollection of how or what happened.

Bridge Near Curecanti

This bridge located across the Gunnison River and upstream from Curecanti on the D&RG's main line between Gunnison and Montrose demonstrates how the Civil War experience of Palmer and his cohorts influenced the building of the line.

Palmer was a cavalryman with some engineering

The fair ladies, and men, arrived at Phantom Curve on Cumbres Pass via an excursion train; they're inspecting the scenic view from that location. In the 1940s the eastbound *San Juan* was struck by a snowslide at this point and part of it went into the canyon below. *W.H. Jackson, Colorado Historical Society*

One of the bridges over the Gunnison River in Black Canyon near Curecanti. Note the unusual construction; looks like rain has washed out the west abutment fill. *W.H. Jackson, Colorado Historical Society*

background. Even before any rail was laid, he began enlisting many of his wartime buddies. Most of the earlier builders and engineers were in this group.

Today this bridge appears unusual, but in the time of road building for wagon traffic in the East, this was of a familiar construction. It was also widely used in building military roads during the Civil War.

The bridge was known as a Howe Arch Bridge and was of the same design as the first bridge built by the Union Pacific over Dale Creek. The bridge trusses are upright triangles anchored to floor girders of heavyweight pieces or laminated sections of wood. The trusses are also tied at the apex of the triangles to a lighter roof girder. After the interrelated components are raised and assembled from the side, the trusses appear as a group of "Xs." Bolted through the girders are vertical steel rods that give added strength to each truss.

At the time (1881-1882), the design was strong enough for heavy farm wagons and for early railroad

equipment and loads, but a decade later, it was not strong enough for railroad equipment and loads. A steel bridge eventually replaced this structure.

Rio de las Animas Canyon

Palmer's track workers and bridge builders hardly had time to recover from their alcoholic headaches, caused by too much drinking at the big bash at Durango on August 5, 1881, celebrating the arrival of the Denver & Rio Grande at Durango, before they were laying rail toward Silverton.

There were no major construction problems until Palmer's crews reached Rockwood, Colorado, but when they proceeded another half mile, the sheer wall of Animas Canyon stopped them on December 11, 1881. Construction was halted until drillers and explosive experts finished blasting a shelf across the face of the cliff at Milepost 470 on the Silverton Branch.

Jackson was the first to shoot a picture of a passenger train on the High Line of the D&RGW's Silverton Branch. Since then railfans have shot hundreds of pictures from the same location down in the canyon and at the same angle, so many that the rocks there are much smoother now. *W.H. Jackson, Colorado Historical Society*

HUMAN GIANTS

Because of impassable terrain on the Animas side of the cliff, the railroad was built to that point. Since the tracklayers could no longer lay rail until the shelf was completed, they worked as muckers for the powder men, blasting the rock and transporting needed material around the mountain from Rockwood to the location where a bridge was built to span the Rio de las Animas Perdidas Canyon. It was so named because of the moaning, groaning and grinding sounds made as the water was forced into the narrow canyon. There was no point in completing the High Line by spring if a bridge was not constructed and ready to meet the point where the grade crossed the river.

Though the High Line and Animas bridge were constructed simultaneously, Palmer's main focus during the winter of 1881-1882 was to blast a shelf across the face of the granite cliff. For those who ride the Silverton train, they will notice images on the face of the cliff at the High Line that look like the sun-god symbol of the Inca and Aztec Indians. These are signs left not by the gods, but by a tribe of human giants who, during

a winter of biting, snow-laden winds and aggravated by working on an exposed rock face, blasted the way for the D&RG to head towards Silverton in the spring. These drillers, powder monkeys and muckers were giants; ordinary men could not have stood up to the demands of the job.

BLACK POWDER

Black powder was used in blasting the High Line, which increased the difficulty of the project. No accurate record dates the arrival of black powder from Asia to Europe, but the first record of its use for blasting dates back to the Royal Hungarian mines in 1627.

Though dynamite had greater applications than black powder for removing large quantities of rock, dynamite could not be transported as safely as black powder until about 1885-1886. By using black powder, Palmer's men had a more tedious and treacherous job blasting a shelf.

SPRAGGING

In blasting the High Line, as at other locations across the country where black powder was used, a method called springing, and known locally as spragging, was used. Spragging involves drilling until enough rock is drilled out to form a hole that can be filled with black powder and ignited.

During this period, the drilling was done by hand using a two-man team. One man held the drill steel in the rock and gave it an eighth of a turn each time the other man hit the drill with a doublejack sledge. Periodically, the pulverized rock was cleaned out of the hole. If a deep hole was needed, it was imperative that the hole be kept round so that the drill continued to turn. This is the reason the drill was never turned more than an eighth of a turn at a time.

When the hole was as deep as required, a small charge was put at the bottom and ignited. This produced a cavity at the bottom of the hole that when cleaned out accepted a larger charge of powder. The cavity and a portion of the drill hole were loaded, a fuse was inserted, and the balance of the hole was tamped with heavy dirt, usually clay. Because the amount of powder placed in the cavity was greater than that which could be placed in a drill hole, the quantity of

rock pulled at each shot was greatly increased. Marks left by these spragged shots formed the sunburst-like images on the wall of the cliff.

Except when shots were fired, a group of expert Italian stonecutters converted pieces of the blasted rock to shapes and dimensions that were used for building walls. Another group of expert Mexican stonecutters later used these ashlars to build crib walls at a few locations where the roadbed could be built without blasting.

CRIBBING

The cribbing could not be done until the manmade shelf was completed. In order to secure the crib walls, it was necessary to drill deep holes in the floor of the new grade in which anchor rods were placed. These anchor rods were handcrafted out of wrought iron with a ringed eye on top and then set in the drill holes. Molten lead was poured in to fill the holes completely to prevent corrosion and seal the rods in the rock.

These anchor rods were set vertically as the cribs were built up. When the desired height was reached, retaining rods were placed down through the protrud-

After the D&RG reached Silverton, it considered it the end of the line, but Otto Mears thought the rich mines near Silverton needed railroads so he built three: Silverton Railroad, Silverton Northern and the Silverton, Gladstone & Northerly. He planned to extend the Silverton on to Ouray, but couldn't find a route to get off the high peaks in the background. Admitting defeat but wanting to reach Ouray, he built a toll road from Silverton to Ouray and the RGS to Ridgway where he connected with the D&RG. There were some mines around Ouray that were almost impossible to reach, except via mule. Such a mule pack train is seen on Main Street, Ouray. *W.H. Jackson, Colorado Historical Society*

54

The *San Juan*, No. 215, at Cumbres in spring of 1950. *M.D. McCarter collection*

ing eyes on the ends of the anchors to form a retaining key for the wall. As the wall was built, rubble from the blasting, along with clay soil hauled from Durango, was deposited behind it to form an airtight and watertight seal.

Since the first train rolled across it, thousands of freight and passenger trains continued to travel the High Line's path. W.H. Jackson was the first to immortalize this scene. Jackson, along with the many photographers who followed, commemorated the exemplary design and wall-building workmanship of the Denver & Rio Grande's Narrow Gauge.

The Pathfinder of the San Juans

When the Civil War ended, men looking for an opportunity to make money returned to the Rocky Mountains, especially to Colorado where there was the promise of wealth from the mines and natural resources.

Of course, any mention of gold or silver strikes quickly drew an interested crowd. But, during the period from 1865 to 1885, the one subject that was never out of anyone's mind was transportation—specifically, railroads.

In Denver when any group of men got together in the evening, their conversations were limited to a few subjects. The importance of the subjects was divided into four categories. The first topic was, "Where shall we eat?" This conversation usually lasted about two to three minutes. The second topic of discussion was,

"Have any new women come to town, and, if so, what do they look like and were they available?" This topic lasted about 10 minutes. The third topic sometimes took 20 minutes to discuss. Deciding whether to patronize the "Circus," Mattie Silks', Jennie Rogers' Mamie Darling's or Fay Stanley's house of pleasure was a hard decision. Once this decision was out of the way, the topic turned to railroads.

With the first three questions out of the way, the group settled back, ordered more cigars and liquor, and got set for discussing the most important subject there was—railroads. Many of these discussions started as the sun went down and were still going strong when its first rays returned to shine on the windows of the meeting room.

OTTO MEARS

There was one individual in southwestern Colorado who was too busy making things happen to join these talk sessions. That was Otto Mears, the "Pathfinder of the San Juans," who came to America from Russia when he was nine years old.

In 1867, Mears ran a store in Saguache, Colorado and experimented with raising grain, especially wheat. About the same time, he was instrumental in bringing about the apprehension of Alferd Packer, the cannibal. He was also editor and publisher of a newspaper and a builder of toll roads including the Saguache to Lake City, Colorado route, which traveled over Cochetopa Pass and on to Ouray; the route over Marshall Pass to Gunnison (later sold to the D&RG for its right-of-way); the route over Independence Pass to Aspen; and, others.

At the outskirts of Ouray, there is a turbulent mountain stream, and flowing into it is a swift tributary running through a cleft in the rock. A bridge is necessary to cross this gap. For those using his toll road between Ouray and Silverton, Otto Mears put a toll house here next to the bridge. Travelers could see into Ouray from here, but until they paid the gatekeeper, they could not go into town. *W.H. Jackson, Colorado Historical Society*

In 1882-1883, Mears built a toll road from Ouray to Silverton, later to be the route of the Million Dollar Highway. On July 8, 1882, the D&RG entered Baker's Park and stopped at Silverton, determined to build no further. Mears was becoming more and more interested in railroads, and, if the D&RG would not build roads up the gulches and valleys around Silverton or up and over Sheridan Pass to the rich deposits at Red Mountain and Ironton, then he would. He also wanted to go to Ouray over this pass with a railroad. His desire to accomplish this amounted almost to an obsession.

GOING AROUND THE MOUNTAIN

In 1887, Mears began building the Silverton Railroad, starting at Silverton, with the avowed intention of extending it to Ouray. By the end of 1888, he built to Chatanooga and Red Mountain. Then he came to Corkscrew Gulch, and it looked as if his progress would have to end. A lot of mine owners and other people between Ouray and Red Mountain were sorely disappointed, but…''By God, and by Otto, they just did not know how tenacious and resourceful this little man was.''

Turntable at Corkscrew Gulch

The covered turntable at Corkscrew Gulch, just above Chatanooga and between Red Mountain and Ironton, was completed on June 14, 1889 and photographed by William H. Jackson shortly before its completion.

The builders were still working on the tail track and the smoke vent of the cone-shaped roof when Jackson shot this photograph. As evident from the photograph, a forest fire occurred a few years prior that allowed Jackson to get a better position for shooting the structure.

Mears did the unusual and built the turntable because there was not enough space to build either a switchback or loop. The turntable is 50 feet long and lies at an elevation about halfway between Chatanooga, which is 10,280 feet, and the summit, which is 11,113 feet. The grade at the turntable was engineered so that gravity would drop the cars into the turntable from either direction.

The engine was run onto it, turned and moved onto a leg of the main track. There was a tail track long enough to hold a car after the engine was turned so that another car could be turned and coupled together with it. When the two were coupled together, the engine was able to reach in for them.

There was nothing unusual about mountain railroads gaining elevation while maintaining a favorable grade, but no railroad builder other than Otto Mears would have thought of building a turntable as part of the main line of his railroad.

Mears built on towards Ouray, but at Alpine, 11.5 air miles from Ouray, the indomitable little giant admitted that he could go no further. All his stubbornness came to the surface: ''If I can't go to Ouray over this mountain, then, by God, I'll go around the mountain.'' He did, and, in doing so, he built the Rio Grande Southern.

Extraordinary isn't even strong enough to describe this scene at Corkscrew Gulch just above Chatanooga. Not enough space for either a switchback or loop, Otto Mears did the unusual but necessary and built a covered turntable. The photo shows two locomotives at the location, which was on the main line of the Silverton Railway. Today only rotting wood pieces remain of the turntable shed and during summer vegetation covers the area so that it's hard to locate, unless you're fairly adept at hiking at upper elevations. *W.H. Jackson, Colorado Historical Society*

Rear end car of the first passenger train through the tunnel passes into the long dark expanse. "No Trespassing" sign was placed there by the D&SL. There was still a lot of cleanup work to be done plus more construction on the venilator building. *Colorado Historical Society*

In 1899, the Silverton went into receivership. In 1904, it was reorganized as the Silverton Railway, still under Mears' leadership. A short time later, the Alpine-Ironton-Red Mountain segment, including the covered turntable, was dismantled because of the impossible operating problems. Operation of the remaining segment lasted until final dismantlement in 1926.

Moffat Tunnel

David Moffat, one of Colorado's great mining figures and railroad builders, organized a standard gauge railroad that went due west from Denver over the Continental Divide to Salt Lake City in 1902. He envisioned as part of this dream a tunnel under the Continental Divide (the main range of the Rocky Mountains). He died on March 18, 1911 without seeing his dream come true, but the idea did not die with him.

His railroad, the Denver, Northwestern & Pacific, was built over Corona Pass at an elevation of 11,000 feet. The route began ascending the pass at Tolland, 47 miles west of Denver, and came off the mountain at

a point near Fraser, Colorado, 62 miles from Denver (modern D&RGW mileposts). Building and operating over Corona Pass required tough, dedicated construction men and railroaders. The Denver, Northwestern & Pacific became the Denver & Salt Lake, then the Denver, Salt Lake & Pacific, and, finally, the Denver & Rio Grande Western acquired the line. To all railroaders and the people of Colorado, it was thought of as the Moffat Road.

As far back as 1911, serious consideration of Moffat's dream arose. The pressure continued until finally in 1922, construction of such a tunnel was approved by the Colorado State Legislature. The tunnel was to be used as a railroad tunnel with an adjacent pilot bore later to be used as a water conduit for western slope water to the eastern slope.

CONSTRUCTION BEGINS

Construction began in mid-1923, and the pilot bored through on February 12, 1927. Work on the railroad portion proceeded from both the west and east ends. Adits (horizontal passage ways) driven from the water bore to the railroad bore expedited work, and the railroad portion was holed through on July 7,

1927. The first Moffat Road train traveled through on February 26, 1928; the first water flowed through in 1936. The water conduit was delayed due to the necessary lining and sealing of the bore against any possible leakage. The first Denver & Rio Grande Western train operated through Moffat Tunnel in June 1934 upon completion of the Dotsero Cutoff.

In building his road from Denver to Tolland, Moffat originally constructed 30 tunnels in a distance of 20 miles, with elevations ranging from 8,866 feet at Tolland to 11,000 feet at Corona Pass. Moffat Tunnel entered the east portal at an elevation of 9,195 feet at Milepost 50.18. The apex at Milepost 52.82 is at an elevation of 9,239 feet; the west portal at Milepost 56.39 is at an elevation of 9,058 feet. The tunnel is 6.21 miles long and is measured from Milepost 50.18 to Milepost 56.39. The cover above the apex measures approximately 4,000 feet passing under James Peak, which is at an elevation of 13,345 feet. In the center of one of the Crater Lakes on the east side of James Peak, there is a small island of white stone reputed to be directly over the apex in the Moffat Tunnel.

In laying out the Moffat Line of the Denver & Salt Lake Railroad, the route first chosen was to go over the mountains from Denver, Colorado, to Craig, Colorado. It was a choice necessitated by financial and technical factors at the time. It was never considered a good choice, and eventually, the portion from Tolland (on the east) to Tabernash (on the west) was abandoned with the completion of the Moffat Tunnel.

As early as 1867, Andrew N. Rogers of Central City, Colorado, published a plan for tunneling under the Continental Divide to Middle Park. In an article appearing in the 1885 *Aspen Sun,* the Burlington Railroad was considering starting a route up Boulder Canyon and into Middle Park and also considered tunneling under James Peak. From 1867, the discussion of such a tunnel was a common attention-getter. No concrete proposals were offered until 1887 when David H. Moffat became involved.

Between 1902 and 1905, the D&SL chipped away at the mountains west of Denver headed toward Salt Lake City. It never reached Salt Lake City, but it eventually reached as far as Craig, Colorado. As part of its plan, Moffat bought the rights of a surveyed line between Kremmling, Colorado to Dotsero on the D&RG. In May 1903, the D&RG's management demanded that Moffat share this possible route with

A Moffat Road freight train struggles upgrade on the mountain near Yankee Doodle Lake. Completion of the Moffat Tunnel eliminated this slow and costly route over Corona Pass. Yankee Doodle Lake is below grade at left center. A tale that is without merit says that a Denver & Salt Lake train derailed at this point, rolled into Yankee Doodle Lake and was never recovered. Through the years Corona Pass has been named Boulder Pass and Rollins Pass. *Colorado Historical Society*

This is Jenny Lake on the Moffat Road looking toward James Peak. Moffat Tunnel went into the eastern base of James Peak at the canyon in left center and under James Peak to emerge at the west portal, Winter Park. *Colorado Historical Society*

Denver & Salt Lake #118, a 2-8-0, was used in making the Westinghouse Air Brake Co. braking tests descending Corona Pass August 21, 1921 described in the text. *Colorado Historical Society*

them. Moffat refused. A portion of the survey was used between Orestod (Bond) on the D&SL and Dotsero on the D&RGW main line to build the Dotsero Cutoff.

Moffat reached Steamboat Springs in 1908 after spending $14 million building his railroad over Rollins Pass at a cost of $75,000 per mile. He died in 1911, almost bankrupt, but still fighting for his dream of a tunnel under James Peak.

PRIVATE FUNDS

A large portion of this money, mostly his private money made from mining, was dissipated in the struggle to operate trains over the 11,000 foot Rollins Pass. The cost of operation was tremendous. It required four Mallet locomotives to boost as few as 22 carloads over the mountain. Adding even one or two more carloads necessitated an additional locomotive. It took between 14 to 16 hours for a freight train to cover the 90 miles from Denver to Tabernash on the west side of the pass. Fighting blizzards and other snow conditions over the years consumed an average of 40 percent of income. Frequently, the Moffat Line could not operate trains for weeks, even months, due to snow blockades.

Moffat was president of the D&RG for a short period, and, during his tenure, he spent $200,000 of D&RG money running surveys involving the line from Kremmling to Dotsero, tunnel feasabilities and westward from Steamboat Springs to Salt Lake City. He was often quoted relative to his plans. His determination to complete the line to Salt Lake City was strong: "I am not content to do nothing. I have decided to build a steam railroad from Denver to Salt Lake City, and it is going to be built."

The paramount requisite to make such a railroad profitable and operable was the tunnel under James

In 1921 Westinghouse Air Brake Co. selected the east side of Corona Pass as being a location where the efficiency of their system could be tested. Engine #118 was used as the locomotive, and a heavy train was coupled behind. The train here has been stopped at Jenny Lake to inspect the results so far in the test. Man in the straw hat is William Freeman, president of the Moffat Road. The automobile was converted to a rail inspection car. *Colorado Historical Society*

This was the scene at the east portal of Moffat Tunnel with the buildings and camp built to house the workers while the tunnel was being drilled. *Colorado Historical Society*

Peak. It would reduce operating elevation about 2,300 feet and track miles about 23 miles while resulting in a much more favorable percentage of grade ascending the east side. Snow conditions would not be eliminated, but they would be more manageable.

Drilling a six-mile tunnel through rock, predominantly granite, was not the primary deterrent; financing was. In 1912 a state bond issuance was passed, but in 1914, Judge George W. Allen ruled it illegal under state law. D&SL went into receivership a second time in 1917. World War I government aid kept it running at a small profit.

Colonel David C. Dodge, a William Jackson Palmer contemporary and associate, became the chief adviser for the drive to build the tunnel. He justified the use of government funds since millions of dollars were spent on the improvements of rivers and harbors, and railroads deserved equal consideration. At the end of World War I, a strong resurgence for a tunnel emerged. Dodge argued the need for land, resources and developing economics would appear with the end of the war. At the time, his arguments were unsuccessful.

The Front Range area, especially metro Denver,

needed to plan for future water supply. The most feasible way to bring water to this area was from the western slope by a tunnel under James Peak. Those pushing for a railroad tunnel gained strong allies.

The Colorado State Railroad Commission was created in 1919, but no money was allocated for its use. This was followed in 1920 by a new tunnel plan aimed at constructing tunnels in D&RGW country under James Peak, Monarch Pass and Cumbres Pass. For some reason, southern Colorado inhabitants opposed this.

In 1922, after a disastrous year of flooding and heavy snowfall, the Pueblo Flood Conservancy and Moffat Tunnel Bill were passed and signed into law. A friendly suit was instituted to eliminate any question of constitutionality in the future.

TUNNELING BEGINS

Constitutionality was confirmed in July 1922. Two months later, the initial cut at the west portal of Moffat Tunnel was made followed shortly by one at the east portal on the Denver side of the Continental Divide. Work progressed steadily and was only delayed in the summer of 1926 by a 125-ton rock slide that killed six men. Some soft rock and water seams were encoun-

These were the living quarters under construction for married workers and families at the west portal of Moffat Tunnel. *Colorado Historical Society*

This is the working site at East Portal of Moffat Tunnel. Lower track leads from adit of tunnel with the upper track and flume and entire system of tracks used for transporting excavated materials which were then dumped in a pattern called the "Big Fill" on which East Portal facilities and wye were later built. *Colorado Historical Society*

Inside of the working face of the west section looking toward the entrance at Moffat Tunnel; the workers are now into granite but water seepage requires the heavy pipe system at left. *Colorado Historical Society*

The first passenger train to go through the Moffat Tunnel was on February 26, 1928. There was still a lot of work to be completed in the wye area, or the tunnel fan and the maintenance crew living quarters. *Colorado Historical Society*

tered, but required only minor special handling in relation to the overall granite in the formation through which the tunnel was drilled.

Early in the morning on February 12, 1927, the hardrock miners of the west portal drove a steel rod into the rock, and it went through into the nothingness of the tunnel from the east portal. A west portal worker put his mouth close to the hole left by the rod and yelled, "Who built this tunnel anyway?" From the east portal crew, a man yelled, "WE built the tunnel."

The west portal crews claimed the honor of making the final opening through the separating rock. They were brought to Denver and treated as heroes. Prohibition was in effect, but when were heroes denied a celebration? In fact, the whole city helped them celebrate. In a little more than three years, the mountain was pierced by crews working from the east and west. The final meeting in the bowels of the earth was incredibly close to perfect alignment.

The citizens of Denver were so happy that they did not take the time to think about the years ahead when they would be paying for Moffat Tunnel. The bond issue specified the D&SL would build to Salt Lake City or the Dotsero Cutoff. It never made it to Salt Lake City.

The Denver radio station KOA covered the driving of the last spike ceremony at East Portal of the Moffat Tunnel. The exact date and the participants are not known, but from the heavy coats it was still mighty cold out; the tunnel bore was completed February 12, 1927.

These are crew quarters at the Moffat Road's sub-terminal at Tabernash, Colorado. They were used for a while by Rio Grande crews after the Moffat Tunnel was completed and the Moffat Road discontinued its line over Corona Pass. *Colorado Historical Society*

The Royal Gorge War

The Press did a lot of muckraking in the West during 1878 and 1879, especially in Colorado reporting on the violent, bloody Royal Gorge War between the Atchison, Topeka & Santa Fe and Denver & Rio Grande railroads.

The reporters did not hesitate to sensationalize news that would sell papers. True, there were fistfights and a few broken skulls and broken bones that resulted when the two railroad opponents swung pickaxe handles and clubs at each other. But even though both railroads provided their men with guns, the men never used them against each other.

The only bloodshed caused by a firearm occurred when a Santa Fe soldier was caught with his pants down by a Rio Grande soldier. When the Rio Grande soldier found his wife entertaining the enemy, the

During the Royal Gorge War, three forts were built and manned by the D&RG. The one in this picture was the first and was named, and a sign was put up which read "Deadline." These men never shot their weapons at the AT&SF men. *W.H. Jackson, Colorado Historical Society*

These are D&RG soldiers in the Royal Gorge War who just arrived in 1878-1879 and are ready to begin building Fort #2, about where Parkdale is now. Fort #1 was downstream from here. Fort #3, a more substantial fort and heavily manned, was at Spikebuck, three miles upstream from Fort #2. *W.H. Jackson, Colorado Historical Society*

This is at Spikebuck, which was the strong point that William Palmer ordered his soldiers to defend to the last ditch. These were a rough, tough group of men, but the ATS&F never got close enough to make it necessary for the D&RG soldiers to fire any shots in anger. In 1879 the so-called war was settled in the courts, and the forts were dismantled. *W.H. Jackson, Colorado Historical Society*

Santa Fe man jumped out of bed, grabbed his clothes and jumped out the window. His pistol fell out of its holster, and the butt of the gun hit the ground and fired. The old, single-action Colts were apt to do this, and the heavy slug tore through the rump of the escaping adulterer.

CHANGING DIRECTIONS

The Santa Fe beat the Rio Grande over the Raton Pass route, so the Rio Grande changed its goals and headed towards Royal Gorge. The Santa Fe was not to be outdone; it headed for Royal Gorge as well.

While the Rio Grande worked at grading inside the Gorge, the Santa Fe, aided by Canyon City residents who disliked General William Jackson Palmer's tactics, built grade at the eastern approach. In an amazing coincidence, both railroads sent out marauding parties the same night. The echoes of the Rio Grande's black powder charges blowing up the Santa Fe's road work hardly died out when similar explosions were heard in the canyon where the Rio Grande's roadbed was. Before the Rio Grande soldiers departed, they threw all

the Santa Fe tools and supplies into the Arkansas River.

The warfare was temporarily halted by court order. A cold war ensued, and Palmer recruited an army of wagoners at Wagon Creek on the west side of La Veta Pass (the current end-of-track) along with other unemployed bullies. The Santa Fe recruited at Dodge City and other Kansas cow towns. Railroad wages determined the loyalty of these recruits, and loyalties changed as each road raised its pay scale.

Palmer built three forts near the upper end of the Gorge. A large sign that read "Dead Line" was posted, and a crude rock and driftwood fort was built at a point where the Arkansas River entered the canyon. Four miles upstream, across the river in the spot where the town of Parkdale, Colorado is now located, a second fort was built and manned. Another three miles from this fort, where Spikebuck siding and a water tank later were located, was the most elaborate, heavily manned fort.

No fighting occurred at either of these forts. In

This is the hanging bridge in the Royal Gorge soon after it was completed; the stone wall used as protection against high water was not yet built. Note that three-rail track had been laid to permit standard gauge trains to Leadville. *W.H. Jackson, Colorado Historical Society*

In this picture in the Royal Gorge the high water control stone wall had been built; hanging bridge design is easily discerned. *W.H. Jackson, Colorado Historical Society*

Again at the Royal Gorge, the third rail has been removed, but not yet filled under the bridge with the later stone-concrete masonry. *Colorado Historical Society*

Engine #1803 and passenger train stop at hanging bridge to allow sightseeing by the passengers. For many years this was a scheduled stop for daylight trains to permit passengers to view the awe-inspiring depth of the gorge. *M.D. McCarter collection*

LEFT. A pretty lass poses for the photographer at the hanging bridge in the Royal Gorge. *Colorado Historical Society*

1879, a final settlement of the dispute was forced by the courts, and the Royal Gorge War ended. The gunmen from the cow towns went home, and the wagoners went back to Wagon Creek and resumed hauling freight to points in the San Luis Valley and the new mining town at Silverton.

The Rio Grande built the Hanging Bridge in the Royal Gorge and then continued west until it reached Leadville in July 1880. From its terminal at South Arkansas, now Salida, it built over Marshall Pass and Poncha Pass to the Gunnison and San Luis valleys, respectively.

The Royal Gorge hanging bridge sightseeing cable car looking up from D&RGW track level to the rim of the gorge. Cable car can be seen at upper left. *M.D. McCarter collection*

An early photo taken by W.H. Jackson showing #228 carrying white flags eastbound in Royal Gorge with a string of flat-bottomed cars loaded with revenue business. *Colorado Historical Society*

The Denver & Rio Grande Western

There has never been a definitive enumeration of the many titles of railroads, railways, transportation and telegraph companies, or the location and segments that were used in the financial wizardy by General William Jackson Palmer during the building of the system that would become the Denver & Rio Grande Western Railroad Company.

There has always been some misconception and erroneous reference in names when alluding to the Rio Grande. It is variously called the Denver and Rio Grande; Rio Grande Western; Rio Grande; D&RG; RGW; and Grande. At some period during the development of the system, any of these titles would have been correct in referring to a specific section. They all finally came together to be the Denver & Rio Grande Western, the *Rio Grande*.

Herbert O. Brayer attempted such an enumeration in his book, *William Blackmore; Early Financing of the Denver & Rio Grande Railway and Ancillary Land Companies, 1871-1878*. This is about as nearly complete as any book on the subject, but it still falls short.

Out of this welter of financial manipulation and trickery came the funds to build a system of three-foot-gauge railroads that connected Denver and Salt Lake City. At the same time, the branch lines stemming from the main trunk that opened the Rocky Mountain Empire were built with money derived from the same schemes. At the time, there were no laws that prohibited any of the practices and quasi-frauds used. Compared to similar methods, plus the outright fraud and thievery used in financing the building of the Union Pacific and Central Pacific, Palmer's actions were almost puritanical.

Eventually from the welter, two railroads emerged. They were the Denver & Rio Grande, which extended west from Denver to the Colorado-Utah state line, and the Rio Grande Western in Utah.

THE CALICO LINE

Utah law specified that any railroad within the state had to have as incorporators at least two-thirds bona fide residents of Utah. Having this knowledge, Palmer secretly began a program of gathering all the small mining railroads in existence in Utah into one system. In 1878, a Milan Packard accomplished this, and the Rio Grande Western was incorporated and given a Utah charter as a railroad to the Colorado-Utah state line. The Rio Grande Western started building east from Salt Lake City. Workers on the first phase of construction took part of their wages in merchandise. A considerable portion of this merchandise consisted of calico for the workers' wives. Locally, the budding railroad was called the Calico Line.

The D&RG leased the RGW in 1882 for a period of 30 years. Neither in Colorado or in Utah was there ever any doubt that both railroads were Palmer's. However, it was never a moot question to anyone.

FORCED OUT

Stockholders and bondholders were dissatisfied with Palmer's policies and actions. On August 9, 1883 he resigned from the D&RG. He then declared ownership and control of the RGW. The 30-year lease between the two roads became a point of conflict.

When Palmer resigned, Frederick Lovejoy was elected president of the D&RG. Lovejoy wanted to break the 30-year lease, and, in an ensuing battle on July 3, 1884, he removed a one-mile section of track just east of the Colorado-Utah state line. The two railroads finally negotiated a truce. The traditional last spike was driven on March 30, 1883, just a few miles west of Green River, Utah.

Lovejoy was defrocked by the stockholders, and, late in February 1885, the D&RG was under the management of William S. Jackson, receiver, and David H. Moffat, president. Peace was declared in 1886, and in 1887, it was apparent that the main route between Denver and Salt Lake City-Ogden had to be standard gauged. Broadening of the gauge was completed in 1890. Some mountain segments were never standard gauged and remained narrow gauge, and some, notably Leadville to Pueblo, operated as three-rail tracks for a while.

Moves to consolidate the two roads began with a meeting held on February 8, 1901. Finally, the railroads were consolidated about 1908. The D&RG paid Palmer $15 million for the RGW. Palmer gave up railroading and retired to Colorado Springs to become that area's greatest philanthropist.

On his farewell trip over the RGW, Palmer gave away $1 million to his loyal employees. The Provo agent reportedly received $35,000. Some say Palmer gave away $3 million. Whatever the amount, Palmer generously thanked his employees.

Green River Valley

The original route of the railroad west of Grand Junction to Salt Lake City left the Grand River Valley at the confluence of East Salt and West Salt creeks. From the creeks near Douglas Pass, the elevation was 8,268 feet; confluence elevation was 4,540 feet. With such a great difference in elevations,

This siding at Utaline, Utah features the state boundary painted on the canyon wall at right. *W.H. Jackson, Colorado Historical Society*

Early day line change and roadbed protection from the Colorado River necessitated using construction equipment of simpler means than what is available today. This picture was taken just west of Mack, Colorado entering Ruby Canyon. *Colorado Historical Society*

severe damage to terrain and any structures along the drainage areas resulted when there were severe rains.

At the confluence, about five miles from where the two streams were known as Salt Creek, the Denver & Rio Grande established a station and named it Mack, Colorado. Fuel and water facilities were established, and a small terminal was built for engines used to help westbound trains from Mack to Hilltop, about 15 miles west of Mack. The route continued up West Salt Creek through Prairie Canyon and reached the flat land at Hilltop. From here, the grade was level all the way to Cisco, Utah.

There was no suitable water supply between Mack and Cisco, so it became necessary to find an alternative route. Not long after the D&RG and RGW met near the Colorado-Utah border to form a through line, surveys were made for a route through Ruby Canyon, on the Colorado River, to Westwater, Utah, at the state line. At Westwater, the survey left the Colorado River, climbed over Cottonwood Hill and traveled on toward Cisco. Construction started later as standard gauge.

Ruby Canyon

The Uintah Railroad on its line and the Rio Grande through Ruby Canyon suffered washouts and flooding at intervals. On the Rio Grande, this was especially severe at the point where the Salt Creek flowed into the Colorado River (originally called the Grand River) and damage usually extended 10 miles downstream.

As a result of one very severe flash flood, the road-bed at the junction of Salt Creek with the Colorado River had extensive damage. The wooden bridge there was washed away, and it eventually was replaced with a concrete bridge over Salt Creek. The railroad was moved to this new grade using the concrete bridge.

The old grade was then left in place to serve as a protective barrier for the new grade. The project was not an urgent one, so work was performed in the most economical way. The Rio Grande's earliest clamshell machine was assigned the job along with a minimal roadway gang. The machine used material from the old grade and some additional material from the river bed. Heavy rocks were used to further protect the river face. At the upper and lower ends of this protective fill,

A work extra on the D&RG on the Blue River branch with a rotary and three locomotives dragging a four-wheel crummy. This is approaching Wortsman, a short distance from Alicante, a distance of 1.22 miles from the summit of Fremont Pass. In the 36.25 miles of this branch line there were 20 sidings or spurs that had operating mines. *Lawrence Gordon Low*

cribs of old rail and fencing wire were built as jetties. Since the completion, there has never been any additional damage.

Blue River

The Royal Gorge War being won, the D&RG built on into Leadville. By the time this occurred, mining north of Leadville to Dillon, Colorado was in high gear. A branchline was started from Leadville to serve the mines north of Leadville. It was called the Blue

River Branch. Construction began in 1881, and the line was opened for business in 1882. The total length of the branch was 36.25 miles, and it was a rugged piece of terrain.

The route went via today's Climax Molybdenum Mine, Wortsman, Alicante, Summit (Fremont Pass), down the Blue River and a number of mine communities to Dillon.

The D&RG operated the branch until 1909 at which time it was leased to the Colorado and Southern that had a branch off its main DSP&P route between

As the three engines and rotary clear a path on the lower loop approaching Wortsman, a couple of men with a horse and sled unload coal from gondolas to be moved to the Wortman Mine to provide power for operations at the mine and for the town itself. *Lawrence Gordon Low*

Denver-Fairplay-Nathrop to Gunnison, Colorado. The rails were removed about 1924, and later, the Colorado and Southern built standard gauge from Leadville to Climax to move the ore produced there.

Some molybdenum remains at Climax, but the operating company discontinued any notable production with the opening of its Henderson Mine near Berthoud Pass, Colorado.

The Blue River area, once nearly as famous as Leadville, is today even more famous for its great ski industry—Copper Mountain, Breckenridge, Keystone, Frisco, Loveland Valley and Dillon. In summer, there is superb fishing, hiking and ghost-towning.

Thousands of tourists close their car windows, turn on the air conditioning in the summer (heaters in the winter), and speed on Interstate 70, which in many places is built on the D&RG's Blue River Branch. Gasoline fumes from automobiles, and smoke and stink from diesel-powered heavy trucks have replaced the smoke of the small narrow gauge engines that once hauled passengers and freight between the historic towns of Leadville and Dillon. The squeal of rubber on asphalt as drivers hit their brakes going into curves too fast is heard where once it was the squeal of train

This snow-bucking train is enroute to Fremont Pass on the Blue River Branch—the pass is about three miles up the line. The Climax molybdenum mine was later opened in this basin. *Lawrence Gordon Low*

wheels negotiating too tight curves laid with 30-pound per yard rail. The peanut roaster whistles of the two teakettle-size engines are replaced by the blare of autos and the Klaxons of speeding trucks.

Hardy miners wielded picks and shovels digging for gold and silver on the Blue River. Now, the natives dig for gold and silver in the pockets of tourists and skiiers.

Engine #484 and caboose #0517 with an Extra East at the high trestle over Wolf Creek at Lobato. *M.D. McCarter collection*

Wolf Creek

Wolf Creek, a tributary of the Chama River, had its source at the head of a grassy sloped valley below Windy Point near the summit of the group of ridges and outcroppings of Cumbres Pass. The rails first crossed it at the bottom of the first steep descent after leaving the Cumbres station. The bridge over the creek at this point was constructed from timber on a sharp curve resembling an elbow. The siding just west of the bridge was named Coxo. In Spanish, "Codo" means elbow, but in the course of mapping the line, the word was incorrectly written, and it was allowed to remain as Coxo.

Wolf Creek ran almost parallel to the railroad track but at a much lower elevation. Nearing its junction with the Chama River, the difference was almost 200 feet below the grade of the railroad. To get across this

chasm, a spidery structure of steel uprights and girders was built. As originally constructed, there was a comfortable margin of safety for the weight of the engines and loads crossing it. As the engines and loads grew heavier, the safety factor decreased, so steps were taken to more closely equalize the weight of the train more evenly along the length of the girders.

A provision in Special TimeTable Rules reads: K-36 and K-37 engines must not be doubleheaded over bridges at Milepost 319.95 and 339.78, Sub-Division 11. The bridge over Wolf Creek was at Milepost 339.78; Milepost 319.95 was on the east side of Cumbres just west of Osier over Cascade Creek.

Nearly all eastbound freight trains leaving Chama required two or more engines to handle the train up the 4 percent grade. When these engines were 480s

This was as famous a picture stop for passengers on the D&RG narrow gauge as Toltec Gorge was on the San Juan extension between Chama and Antonito. It's Chipeta Falls at the Black Canyon of the Gunnison River. *Colorado Historical Society*

or 490s (or a combination of them), the train was made up at Chama with a minimum of five freight cars between the engines. More commonly, the second, but sometimes the third, engine was trained at the rear of the train just ahead of the caboose.

There was no problem for westbound trains because descending required no additional power. There was a problem in the winter using the rotary snowplow, which was as heavy or heavier than a K-36 or K-37 engine. In operating the rotary under working conditions, an engine was needed behind the plow to move it and keep it up against the snow.

When plowing eastward leaving Chama, the extra fuel cars and crew cars were trained behind the rotary plow and kept that way until Cresco, four miles east of the bridge. At that point, the engine was properly trained behind the plow. A westward plowing job lined up cars behind the rotary at Cresco and kept them in this position into Chama.

The Chama River flowed in a rocky gorge from the confluence of Wolf Creek and this river paralleled the railroad beyond the bridge, and much below, track level. Lobato siding was in close proximity to the west end of the bridge. Across the canyon, there was an aspen-clad mountain that in autumn presented a picture of breathtaking beauty. The autumn leaves here turned the brightest red of any other location on the entire Narrow Gauge. People came from Denver and other points to ride the passenger trains to see this beautiful scene.

My fondest remembrances of this bridge are of the many days I spent fishing above the bridge in Wolf Creek with the solitude, stillness and abundance of cutthroat trout found there.

Overturned passenger train on the Leadville-Dillon (Blue River Branch) west of today's Officer Campground near Frisco, Colorado. The line was built between 1881-1882 and the last of operations was in 1909; the tracks were pulled up in 1924, after being leased for a while to the Colorado & Southern. *M.D. McCarter collection*

Chapter 4

Natural and Manmade Disasters

Passenger Train Derailments

On the Narrow Gauge, there were surprisingly few memorable passenger train wrecks. There was no information about this wreck, but looking at the photograph closely, I believe that the accident occurred on the D&RG's Blue River Branch that ran from Leadville to Dillon, Colorado, near a station named Wheeler.

Wheeler was between Kokomo and Dillon, about two miles north of the junction of Highway I-70 and State 91 at Copper Mountain, and about a mile south of Officer's Campground. This is the only location on the Narrow Gauge periphery that fits the picture. Ten Mile Creek is to the right of this railroad and is a tributary of Blue River. At this point, Highway I-70 is parallel to the creek.

Many interesting features in the photograph support the fact that this derailment happened at an early date:

- The type of engine in the background.
- The wheel mark of a derailment inside the righthand rail.
- The broken socket of a link and pin coupling on the rear coach, and dangling chains used to supplement that link and pin coupling.
- Four-hole anglebars with only two bolts used.
- Rails spiked to hewed pole ties, only one spike at each spiking location.

- Roadbed laid on natural surface, no ballast.
- No airbrake cylinders, indicating no airbrakes of any type.
- Ties are "pole ties" cut near the right-of-way from 6- to 8-inch trees, peeled and flattened on two sides with a broadaxe, then hacked, not sawed, to length.

All indications are that the train overturned from excessive speed.

Kokomo is at an elevation of 10,614 feet and 18.43 miles from Leadville. The next major station was at Wheeler, which was at an elevation of 9,781 feet and 22.69 miles from Leadville. The fall in grade in this section was 833 feet in 6.3 miles, for an average descending grade of a little more than 3 percent. This was steep and probably the cause of the wreck.

OTHER PASSENGER TRAIN DERAILMENTS

A special train carrying dignitaries en route to a celebration of the Rio Grande reaching Durango wrecked near Toltec Gorge. Shortly after, on August 4, 1881 and approximately at the same location, a passenger train wrecked, killing eight people and injuring six. In January 1918, the *Millionaire Special,* a train carrying financiers interested in the Silverton mines, struck a snowslide and wrecked. No one was hurt, but business cars B and N burned. On July 17, 1929 Train No. 425 en route to Santa Fe ran away on Barranca Hill and wrecked. Many fatalities occurred.

Then there was the headend to rearend collision just east of Monero involving a snowplow train and Train No. 116. There were no injuries. Train No. 116, the eastbound *San Juan,* was involved in another accident. It was struck by a snowslide at Phantom Curve on Cumbres Pass, and two people were injured, but there were no fatalities.

Jackknifing produced this derailment of a D&RGW coal train on the Sunnyside Branch. The train had made a pickup of Carbon County Railroad coal and was leaving Columbia Junction when the derailment occurred.

This test train with Electro-Motive test car between two sets of power units ran between Castlegate and Royal, Utah. The Geeps are up front and the F unit diesels behind the test car.

Jackknifing Standard Gauge Trains

When I transferred to Helper, Utah, in June 1953 as trainmaster, I quickly learned that the most pressing problem was rerailing coal trains derailed between Helper and Soldier Summit, with some occurring on the Sunnyside Branch. The Union Pacific was having the same type of derailments with the iron and coal trains in the Provo area.

The derailments on the Rio Grande started soon after the coal movements were totally dieselized. Dieselization permitted hauling heavier and longer trains upgrade, and improved braking capability permitted these same trains to descend safely from Soldier Summit to Gilluly.

It was not unusual to have more than one derailment in a 24-hour period. Usually, equipment damage was minimal, and the track was repaired in the course of rerailing. There were many shipments of coal and other commodities, and each derailment delayed both scheduled and extra movements.

G.B. (Gus) Aydelott, who later became the Rio Grande's president, was superintendent at Salt Lake City. Finding a solution to these jackknifings was my number one priority. The Union Pacific was having similar problems, so we visited some of its derailments, and Union Pacific officials visited some of ours.

TESTING BEGINS

The Association of American Railroads (AAR) was interested in these derailments and sent a crew, along with an Electro-Motive test car and a large collection of stress-gauging equipment, to Helper to study the derailments. The testing program lasted for 10 days, and, during this time, we did everything we could think of to pinpoint the cause. On the 10th day, we had thousands of stress readings and other information, but no solution to the problem.

We did notice a reoccurring trend on the Sunnyside Branch: all the derailments occurred shortly after the train left Columbia Junction. When we reviewed the events immediately prior to the derailments, we found that the jackknifings occurred after the first application of the airbrakes.

At the moment of application, most of the train was still on the flat and the brakes were fully released. One of our road foremen of equipment was knowledgeable about airbrakes and surmised that the train line air did not immediately "dump" the length of the train.

Consequently, when the airbrakes were applied on the lead engine, the front part of the train was on the grade, but the middle and rear cars were not on the grade and still moved freely. Because the airbrakes did not affect the rear cars in time, the rear cars ran into the lead cars and caused them to jackknife.

There was a section of grade leaving Columbia Junction that required the use of airbrakes, so the foreman ran a series of braking experiments and found that by pulling the entire train over the hump with the

The Electro-Motive test car at Helper, Utah.

brakes set only to a certain degree, it would not derail. His experiments were successful, and there never were any more jackknifings because of airbrakes on the Sunnyside Branch.

MORE PROBLEMS

Though the problem was solved for the Sunnyside Branch, we continued to have derailments going uphill, usually between Royal and Kyune, Utah. Aydelott came to Helper determined to find a solution.

We reviewed many accident reports, queried train and engine crews and did a lot of brainstorming. We rode on each of the coal train's locomotives and cabooses and followed along the highway observing the train in action. During this period, there was not one derailment, but this was illogical since we did not make any changes in the train makeup or positioning of helper engines.

The standard practice was to position the first helper engine behind the tonnage rating of the train's engine. At Kyune, where the grade flattened, one helper engine was cut out to return to Helper.

While the written accident reports did not reflect it, our discussions with crew members revealed a pattern: in each derailment, the lead engine applied the airbrakes. Apparently, it was Sunnyside Branch all over again—slow-moving train air.

These were long trains, and there was no form of communication between the lead engine and helper engines. The only indication on the helper engines that the lead engine had applied the airbrakes was when the air pressure gauge fell. When the engineers on the helper engines noticed this drop, they made the

appropriate power reductions on their engines. Human reaction and brake action were not instantaneous, so each helper was still pushing against the cars ahead of that engine with the brakes set. Jackknifing then occurred somewhere between the middle and rear helpers and usually involved two to eight cars.

MORE TESTING

We needed a derailment to test this theory, but there were none at the time. Hoping to find a solution to the problem, we decided to cause a derailment. We knew that the Interstate Commerce Commission (ICC) would reprimand us for an intentional derailment, but we went ahead anyway and did not worry about the consequences.

On the day of the test, a normal coal train was assembled. A road foreman of equipment was at the throttle on each locomotive. The foreman on the lead engine was told that at some point around a curve, he would see a white flag and should immediately proceed to stop. The other two foremen were instructed to watch their air pressure gauges constantly, and, at the first indication of a reduction, they were to take the usual action of reducing power.

President Aydelott and I, along with others, stood at the point that we estimated the lead engine would start applying the airbrakes. I was equipped with a hand-held movie camera to take pictures beginning at the middle engine's nose when the lead engine applied the airbrakes.

When the lead foreman noticed the flag, he set the brakes, and I started filming. About 10 cars behind the first cut-in helper engine, the rear end of a car began to

Standard gauge locomotive #3363, a 2-6-6-0, was classified as an L-77. The large articulated engines of this class had tractive power of about 76,400 pounds, superheaters and power reverse gear. The 2-6-6-0s were formerly of the Denver & Salt Lake, and the D&RGW received 16 of them when the two roads merged in 1947.

This 2-8-0 #318 is one of the five D&RG locomotives of the C-18 Class featuring 38" drivers. *Colorado Historical Society*

THE DENVER AND RIO GRANDE R. R. CO.

Engine No. _10_ Date _6-27-19-16_ 191_

| Train | FROM | TO | MILES | | | | Time Departed | Time Arrived | Hours on Road | Delayed Time |
			Regular	Helper	Light	Mixed				
X	Ouda	Dallas Deude	14				945ᵃ	1205ᵖ	220	35
X	Dallas Deude	Prdg	13				1220ᵖ	120ᵖ	1	0

Called for Train __E X__ to leave at __945 am__ Overtime claimed __1__

Always Explain "Work."   _G. Talbert_ 8 5 0 Engineer.

Always Explain Delays on Back.   _Archey McClellan_ 33 Fireman.

Engine #3607 on the D&RGW standard gauge line; it was of the Class L-131. Taken at Minturn, Colorado, September 4, 1954. *M.D. McCarter collection*

Engine #482 at Alamosa in June of 1959. *M.D. McCarter collection*

The line is attached to engine #473 to pull from her the Animas River after she hit a sunkink in mid-July and dove into the fast-rushing stream. The accident caused problems.

jackknife, and six more followed before the train stopped.

The film was developed within 48 hours, and we sat and watched it over and over again. There was no doubt as to what happened. The middle engineer noticed the air reduction and set his airbrakes. The rear engine, still in motion, never received any indication of the reduction before the train line separated. The first indication that this happened was when the air pressure went to emergency as the derailed cars separated.

After exhaustive discussions about tractive effort, the absence of communication between engineers and the rate of air flow reduction along the train, we experimented putting one engine behind two tonnage ratings, with the second helper engine coupled to the first and pulling its tonnage. This helper arrangement solved our jackknifing problems, but the ICC was fumed and gave the Rio Grande a written reprimand.

Later, it assisted us and the AAR in making additional tests.

My Training as a Dispatcher

My training as a dispatcher began at Alamosa early in 1942. World War II was on the horizon, and the Rio Grande was training men at each dispatching office. Leonard H. Hale was the Inspector of Transportaion and responsible for training and qualifying dispatchers. He was also my father's close friend who made arrangements for me to work a few days at the Alamosa "RM" (Morse call letters for dispatcher at Alamosa) office in order to get my seniority date ahead of the other students.

I had three days of dispatching experience when an emergency arose at Salida, and Hale ordered me there to fill the gap. With only token experience, it was with trepidation that I agreed to do so.

A Class K-36 #484 built by Baldwin in 1925 eases its load of box cars and gondolas through the Colorado mountains near Los Pinos. The Colorado sun casts dark shadows here and there to highlight the locomotive in this dramatic photo taken by Chris Burritt.

"The Silverton" gets ready to depart Durango in the mid-1960s with K-28 #476. Worker and engineer chat prior to pulling out with a couple of gondolas of pipe, and a string of passenger cars to accommodate the tourist trade. *Lee Monroe*

A K-37 Mikado power parade gets ready for work near the turntable in Durango in July of 1959. *Lee Monroe*

#493 K-37 gives a powerful push to a freight train near Cresco. Caboose #04343 tags along behind the locomotive. *Chris Burritt*

K-28 #473 with a work extra to Silverton sits quietly at Elk Park wye in late July, 1959. Photographer Lee Monroe was also fireman on this run; Jim Pearce was engineer.

F7 #5724, a 1,500 hp diesel unit with freight train, has entered Salida, Colorado and is awaiting a crew change. Salida, located between the forks of the Arkansas River, was important to the Rio Grande; a large roundhouse and station once graced the right-of-way in town. *Charles Zeiler*

Lumber and empty flats make up a good portion of this extra train flying along the "race track" towards Alamosa in June, 1959. *Lee Monroe*

K-37 #497 is ready for service at Durango; the white billowy clouds in the background provide contrast to the black boiler of the locomotive. *Lee Monroe*

Classes K-36 (#484) and K-37 (#492) team up on a freight train sometime in the 1960s. If you look closely you can see the railroad sign of Oxford in front of the second locomotive's stack. *Chris Burritt*

"Wild Bill" Holt oils around #499, a 2-8-2 K-37 prior to coupling the engine to his extra train and heading for Durango in August of 1959. *Lee Monroe*

One of the beautiful PA1s is in charge of a passenger train at Denver Union Station. The 2,000 hp PAs were built by Alco in 1947. Some were later sold for scrap, traded to EMD or converted to steam generator cars. *Chris Burritt*

#493 is breathing fire and smoke in an effort to get under way with a freight train that will deliver needed goods to industries on-line in Rio Grande country. *Chris Burritt*

The morning I reported at Salida, I was on the platform in front of the office when an eastbound freight pulled down the main line. On the nose was a 2-8-8-2 L-131, and it looked as big as a battleship.

My trepidation became more like incipient panic. I could imagine the horrible mess if I made an error with a lap order and headed two of these monsters together. Prior to seeing this great pile of iron, all my experience on the Narrow Gauge was dispatching C-Class and K-Class motive power. At Alamosa, I saw the smaller power used between Pueblo and Alamosa including a few Mallets of the 3300, 3400 and 3500 size, but nothing like that giant 2-8-8-2.

I did take over a trick on the graveyard tour, and, for the first 30 days, I did not tie up the railroad or cause any major delays. The night chief, Max Hansen, helped me along at times, but I started to get a bit cocky.

NEAR MISS

Then one morning, about an hour after taking the transfer from the dispatcher I was relieving, I went through a traumatic experience that every old train order dispatcher (if he tells the truth) went through at least once in his career.

A westbound freight dropped its helper engine at Tennessee Pass to return light to Salida. I gave the operator at Tennessee Pass a straight running order for the engine from Tennessee Pass to Salida. Only a few minutes later, the speaker announced "OS Tennessee Pass." (A train report to follow.)

My head exploded for it was only then that I remembered there was a second westbound freight about 12 to 15 minutes away from Malta. Neither of these trains had any information about the other; they would both occupy that single track and keep rolling until they crashed into each other.

Fortunately, the brass pounder at Malta was listening and answered immediately when I said, "Malta" into my transmitter. I told him to grab a fusee and run to the west switch, open it and light the red. The man was one of the old-timers, and he got to the west switch, opened it and broke out the red fusee just as the light engine came around the curve about a mile west of Malta. The engine driver was alert and got enough sand and air under the wheels to go through the open switch at a speed only a bit over the allowable limit.

He pulled further down the siding and dimmed his headlight just as the westbound engine was about a half a mile from the east switch. After registering at Salida, the light engine's jockey came to my office. I expected him to tear me apart, but instead, he just stood and looked at me for a while, then said, "Son, you just put a lot of good men in danger tonight. From now on, be careful."

After completing my trick, I went to Harry Egly, chief dispatcher, and confessed, expecting him to fire me. Egly was an unexcitable soul. He listened to my tale, then told me to sit down. Although a busy man, he spent about 30 minutes calming me down and talking about the hazards and responsibilities a train dispatcher faced every minute he was on duty, and the often nerve-shattering things each of them faced at intervals during their careers.

No, he did not fire me, and he hardly raised his voice until the very end. As I was getting up to leave, so did Egly. He slammed his fist on the table and yelled, "Don't you EVER put out an order or clear a train until you doublecheck both sides of the train sheet, east and west, the orders transferred to you and any branch junctions a train can come from."

Egly and I had a relationship of some kind for many years after that. He never once reminded me of my first lap order mishap, and I hardly ever heard him yell again. He got his message across to me loud and clear.

Pulling Engine No. 473 out of the Animas River

During June and July of 1951, Nat Holt was filming that excellent railroad film, *Rio Grande,* on the Silverton Branch. We supplied two quasi-operative C-Class engines, No. 319 and one other old C-18, which were due for scrapping, to be used in an actual head-on collision.

The collision scene was to be shot on July 16 or 17. The D&RGW was feverishly working to get all business out of Silverton ahead of the collision date. Then on July 11, Engine No. 473 hit a sun kink on the curve at Milepost 483.75 and nosed into the Animas River with 900 tons of concentrates against its rear coupler. We had problems.

Utilizing all the tricks of the trade and every vestige of natural light, we were ready for the final pull at noon on July 15. The cables drew taut, the deadman held, and the winch on the D-7 Cat kept winding and winding. Engine No. 473 came to grade. After rebuilding the track, we checked Engine No. 473 and coupled it to Engine No. 478, then headed for Durango.

Holt got his collision on time, but the Interstate Commerce Commission (ICC) was enraged about it and burned our tails with a written reprimand. Even though no one was on either engine at the time of impact, and safety measures along with protective screens were used, the ICC was infuriated. The motion picture is a classic, and whoever worried about the ICC?

On his first tour of the D&RGW, President G.B. Aydelott's business car caught fire, perhaps from insulation overheating. There were no injuries, but part of the car's table silver melted together. This picture was taken at Cisco, Utah where the car was set out and fire extinguished.

Fire on Business Car 105

G.B. (Gus) Aydelott's long and distinguished career as president of the Rio Grande almost ended on his first tour of the line as president.

The Burnham Shops rushed the restoration of business car #105 so that it would be ready for Aydelott's tour. Aydelott and his family were traveling in the car when, shortly after leaving Westwater, one of Aydelott's family members was awakened by the smell of smoke. The train crew was notified, and arrangements were made to set out the car at Cisco, Utah. Aydelott's family transferred to the Pullman and proceeded to Salt Lake City.

At the time, I was trainmaster at Grand Junction, and we assembled a crew of car department employees to extinguish the fire. The walls of car #105 were full of synthetic insulation that either had been smol-

Fire and smoke damage to Business Car #105 is clearly visible in this scene at Cisco, Utah. On-board personnel were awakened and evacuated from the car; there was extensive damage.

dering for some time or caught fire from static electricity. During this period, we were having trouble with fires occurring in the insulation of our refrigeration cars, too.

Fortunately, damage to the car was more from the heat than flames. Indicative of the heat generated by the fire was the fact that all the table silver along with several pieces of silver plate, which were in a cabinet drawer near the center of the fire, melted together. Though the damage was extensive, the fire did not destroy the body of the car.

The Silverton Branch

The Silverton Branch was built from Tacoma to Silverton, close to the Animas River, through a series of very narrow canyons with steep walls of almost bare rock on each side of the river. It suffered a number of floods so severe that they were remembered and chronicled.

The most remembered floods occurred in 1905, 1911, 1915, 1923 and 1970. Each flood wiped out miles of roadbed and washed ties and rails away. The force of the waters was so great that it left behind twisted rails in many locations, and, in this particular case, it supposedly drove the rail through a tree. Close examination shows that the rail is only resting on the splinters of the tree, which was previously broken off and the top washed away.

There are other controversies presented by this photograph. Lucius Beebe, in Bulletin 67A, *the Narrow Gauge Railroads of Colorado* (page 43), states that this was the flood of 1915 and that it is a 70-pound rail stuck in the tree. In 1915, there was no 70-pound rail on the Silverton Branch. A number of copies of this picture from the Doris Wilson collection date this incident as the flood of 1923.

The Silverton Branch was originally 40-pound rail, which wore badly, and within a few years, was replaced by 52-pound rail. The next predominant weight was 65-pound and was laid during 1929-1930. To expedite restoration of the railroad after the wipe-out flood of 1911, new 90-pound rail was laid between Milepost 476.93 and Milepost 481.47. After the flood of 1923, a mile of washed-away rail between Mileposts 484.34 and 485.38 was replaced with secondhand 85-pound rail.

As needed, some rail in the 80- to 90-pound categories replaced lighter rail. No 70-pound rail was ever used. In 1963 when the railfan era began, a serious relay rail project started, especially from Rockwood into Silverton; most of the rail was either 85- or 90-pound secondhand. As late as 1966, the rail weight from Durango to Tacoma was 65-pound. One short piece of station track at Tacoma was found to be 30-pound; much of the track at the Silverton yard was 52-pound rail.

THE FLOOD OF 1911

The most devastating flood was the one that occurred in 1911 when torrential rains in early November soaked an early snowfall. The D&RG lost miles of main line track along the San Juan River from its

Debris left by the 1923 Animas Canyon flood. Note where the rail went through the tree before the tree broke and was washed away. Nature's fury sometimes is more than a person would believe. *Colorado Historical Society*

The day following Labor Day, 1970, there was a devastating flood on the Silverton Branch near Needleton Siding. I was sent to investigate (that's my backpack in the picture). There was no other way to get into the flood area except on foot, and there were no accommodations except what I carried on my back. This was a dangerous assignment, but I still enjoyed it because I was all alone with the wilderness and the wild animals.

This is Cumbres Yard after the Big Storm. Brake staffs are all that show on the box and refrigerator cars. The Cumbres telegraph office roof and semaphore peek out at upper left of photo.

confluence with the Navajo River near Juanita, and Arboles, Colorado. The D&RG was so busy trying to restore this track that it could not fully attend to the Silverton Branch. Otto Mears made available all his men and equipment, and it truthfully can be said that he and his men were responsible for reopening the Silverton Branch in such good condition.

THE FLOOD OF 1970

The flood of 1970 occurred on Labor Day and closed down railfan train service until the following tourist season. While I was evaluating the damage caused along the shelf just upstream from Tacoma (where the railroad was restored from the three previous floods), I found several of the crib sections, used in previous restorations, rotted, but still recognizable and in place. The railroad was restored in the previous floods by a long crib of pine logs filled with rubble and later buried under ballast.

In a section of this old cribbing and protected by some rocks, a piece of rotting tree trunk was imbedded in it. Parallel to its horizontal length was a piece of rusted rail. When I scoured the rail with sand, it read, "...ron Works—1878." I could not decipher the first word, but I assumed that "ron" stood for "Iron."

The *San Juan*, Snow and Cumbres Pass

Passenger service between Salida and Gunnison, Colorado was discontinued on November 24, 1940, and the cars were moved to Alamosa to be used on the *San Juan* trains, Nos. 215 and 216. They continued to be used for the remaining 10 years of Rio Grande narrow gauge passenger service.

When the narrow gauge passenger equipment was

These are the kind of snowdrifts found near Tanglefoot Curve where the two snowsheds are located on the following page. I took this photo in January, 1952 on a snowshoe reconnaissance mission ahead of the rotary outfit.

refurbished in 1937, some cars were assigned to the Marshall Pass route, and others were assigned to the Cumbres Pass route. The train that ran between Salida and Gunnison was christened the *Shavano;* the train that ran between Alamosa and Durango was named the *San Juan.* The illuminated medallion on the rear car of the *Shavano* was not removed when it was transferred to Alamosa. For the following 10 years when this car was used on the *San Juan,* the rear of the train carried the *Shavano* medallion.

By the mid-1940s, Cumbres was only intermittently established as a telegraph and train order office, usually during the livestock season from September 1-November 30. When there was no operator assigned, the arms of the semaphore train order signal were removed to indicate that the station was closed. Another indication that the Rio Grande never intended to reopen Cumbres is that the shingles on the roof of the privy were not repaired. When Cumbres was open all year, a tightly roofed privy was imperative. During the winter months, drifting snow piled up so high that the lower windows of the depot, along with the station sign, were buried. When this happened, the entire structure of the agent's privy was also buried. After a heavy snowstorm, the section men's first duty was to shovel a pathway to the privy. Quite often, a tunnel was needed.

This is Tanglefoot Curve just east of the summit at Cumbres. Timber has not yet grown back from the great Osier forest fire that denuded the area in 1879. Note the trestle over Cumbres Creek, later filled, and two snowsheds and the second trestle east of the easternmost shed, later filled in. After the timber returned, the sheds weren't needed, but this segment received the greatest drifts each year as anywhere on Cumbres and required the heaviest rotary snowplow work. *W.H. Jackson, Colorado Historical Society*

THE SNOWSTORM OF 1952

The winters at Cumbres Pass were unpredictable. Some winters, snowfighting equipment sat at terminals waiting and was not needed. During others, it was not unusual to experience a snowfall of as much as 500 inches.

The granddaddy of all snowstorms on Cumbres Pass occurred during the winter of 1951-1952 and became the gauge by which previous and future snowstorms were / are measured.

We whipped the first round of the 1951-52 storm, so the snowfighting equipment was sent back to Alamosa just before midnight on January 12, 1952.

Norman Baughman, the bulldozer operator, Joe Rael, the section foreman, and two section laborers were left at Cumbres. They never anticipated another snowstorm that year that would close the Pass again.

On January 15, the weathermen reported that another snowstorm was about to hit in a few days. We prepared the rotary OY and departed Alamosa at 3:45 a.m. on January 16 in order to get a jump on the storm. The men at Cumbres were in no danger because they were experienced Cumbres Pass men, and they also had plenty of fuel and food.

What did worry us was that there was no backup for the rotary OY. After returning from the bout with the first storm, the rotary OM was sent to the backshops for heavy repairs.

The storm broke on January 17, and it was worse than the first one. After more than the usual delays and tribulations, we reached Milepost 328, which is about three miles from Cumbres. There was a lot of snow ahead, and we were running low on fuel and food. An air drop at Milepost 328 on January 25 restocked our food supply, but the need for fuel was critical, and the nearest supply was at Cumbres.

After breakfast on January 26, I left the rotary outfit at Milepost 328 and used snowshoes to trudge through the snow toward Cumbres. When I got there, I found the lumber cars set out by an earlier Chama-Cumbres Turn almost buried in drifted snow, and the coal cars were east of these.

When I went to the section house, I found the snowbound men sitting around the table drinking coffee. I shared some coffee with them before we started working.

CLEARING THE WAY

I assigned Baughman and his bulldozer along with the section men to clear snow along one side of the lumber and coal cars and clear a path to the point where the upper and middle loops of Tanglefoot Curve were closest together. We used the bulldozer to move the lumber from the cars to this point. When that was done, we dumped a car of coal and began tramming it to the same point using the bulldozer blade as a bucket.

I explained to them that T.J. Cummins, road foreman of equipment, thought he could make it to this point with the remaining fuel available to the rotary train locomotives and the rotary. Once at this point, we would have to build a chute on top of the snow and let gravity drop the coal to the engines and rotary on the lower loop.

The Cumbres men did their part, and with Cummins watching every scoop of coal that the firemen used, the rotary got to the desired point. A wooden chute was built, and the coal was slid down into the tenders. Once again, we had steam on all the engines and rotary.

From January 12, 1952 to January 16, 1952, 14 feet of snow fell. Overall, 480 inches (40 feet) of snow fell during the 1951-1952 season.

As darkness fell on January 29, we rolled across the Chama River bridge, near the east end of Chama's yard, with all whistles blasting, even on the rotary OY.

Not much nightlife—or anything else—here at Big Horn sectionhouse on the Cumbres Route. During the snow blockade of 1952, section men from Osier and Sublette took refuge here and tore out floors for firewood. *W.H. Jackson, Colorado Historical Society*

Wreck at Green River: the Mormons Lend a Hand

Several of my friends who were firemen agree that the greatest hazard and aggravation during the course of fighting a fire is the public that is drawn to the scene. If the public is drawn to watch a blazing building, it is drawn more strongly to a train wreck.

As important as a competent, experienced wrecking foreman at a wreck, were members of our security division. They were there to some extent to prevent pilferage, but their primary responsibility was to keep outsiders away, as tactfully as possibly, otherwise forcefully.

I remember one wreck in November 1954 when this was not so. A burned off journal on a car in an eastbound train as it rounded the curve near the Green River depot resulted in a massive pile-up just short of the west end of the bridge over the Green River. Cars were shattered and piled up four high on the rail structure and in tangled wreckage on both sides of the high fill of the bridge approach.

I was just transferred to Grand Junction as trainmaster under Superintendent L.B. Coleman. Upon receiving notice of the wreck, we took off by automobile, with Coleman driving at his usual 90 mph. Coming over the last hill east of Green River, the wreck was in clear sight. It was awesome. Fortunately, there was no smoke, which indicated that there was no fire. There were no tank cars, so there was no possibility of leaking chemicals, either.

HELP ON THE WAY

Wrecker derricks were on their way from Grand Junction and Helper, Utah, plus additional forces were arriving by truck and automobiles. After evaluating the

That tense moment when the Big Hook starts pulling; that's D&RGW derrick #020.

situation and reaching an estimate of the date the track would be reopened for service, Coleman went to the depot. He discussed the matter with the Denver office and made further arrangements to detour the trains. He also ordered two heavy bulldozers to be rushed to Green River by flatbed truck. All section forces as far west as Price, Utah and Mack, Colorado were ordered to Green River.

It was apparent from the large displacement of fill that a lot of new fill and ballast was needed. This was ordered to be shipped from the Murray, Utah slag pile (the D&RGW previously bought this pile) to the wreck.

Because of the badly shattered condition of the cars and lading, especially several carloads of finished lumber, a great deal of plain old manual labor was needed, but we did not have enough people to rapidly clear the wreck. Green River was not a large town, but some spectators started to gather.

A tall, gangling farmer-type approached me, and I was getting ready to tell him to get out of the way when he informed me that he could have at least 100 hard workers on the scene in two to three hours. He continued by saying that their wives would be close behind them to feed the workers, including ours if necessary.

The gentleman did not introduce himself, but I began to get an inkling that he represented members of the Church of Latter Day Saints (Mormons) in the area. His offer could answer our need, so I inquired what the cost would be. These laborers would work as long as needed in return for all undamaged lumber and any other usable building material plus all food items including a carload of sugar, two cars of canned milk and one car of canned goods. He requested anything considered of value for use in their Stakehouse Program, which was equivalent to other faiths' churches.

All the items he named were in cars more or less damaged, and I explained that some of the food items might be contaminated. He replied that the Church had competent people to sort the food.

110

Representatives of our Claims Department arrived, so I had them and Coleman discuss this proposition. A deal was struck, and, almost immediately, some men from the crowd were ready to work.

Soon after, women and elderly men were busy in the grove of cottonwood trees along the river just north of the wreck. Long tables made of lumber from the wreck and a few wood-burning stoves and grills for pit fires were set up. There was an abundance of food, and soon the smell of coffee along with other aromas was in the air and overrode the smells coming from the wreck.

On a couple of occasions, I made it a point to visit the kitchen area. Those Mormon women were excellent cooks, and others of our work force agreed.

This was one time we were not bothered by spectators because that Mormon elder saw to it that anyone who got near the wreck worked.

During this period, there were many jackknifings between Royal and Kyune, Utah, but we were not bothered by sightseers because the wrecks occurred down in Price River Canyon, and the highway was high up on the wall with no trails into the canyon.

THE NARROW GAUGE

There were not many spectators when derailments happened on the Narrow Gauge. Of course, we never had *wrecks* on the Narrow Gauge, but a few were just a bit more than derailments. A factor that made them less stressful was that cleanup was less urgent. If there was a problem that the train and engine crew could not handle themselves, preparations for cleanup were at a leisurely pace. The major worry when taking the tool cars out to pick up a narrow gauge derailment was whether the cook on the kitchen car would select large, tender beefsteaks.

I was involved with matters on the Narrow Gauge from mid-1937 until the rails were pulled up. During that time, there was only one incident where urgency was required. That incident occurred on February 11, 1948 when I was chief dispatcher at Alamosa. The eastbound *San Juan* was struck by a snowslide near Phantom Curve on Cumbres Pass. Passengers were involved, and there was a possibility of injuries, including frostbite.

On that occasion, we had a relief train with a doctor on board, which departed Alamosa in about an hour after the wreck. Upon arrival at the scene, all passengers were covered with blankets. The brakeman sustained cracked ribs; the conductor sustained a lacerated scalp; and the parlor car attendant sustained lacerated legs. The injured crew members and passengers were brought to Alamosa by the relief train. The track was not damaged, so we took our time getting the passenger cars out of Toltec Gorge.

Castlegate, Utah Flood of 1917

The Price River, as it flows eastward from the Soldier Summit drainage area is relatively a slow flowing stream until it enters the canyon at Kyune. The

The scene at Castlegate, Utah in June of 1917.

The Price River, with its tremendous velocity, caused this yard trackage at Castlegate to buckle.

area drained is large, and during heavy seasonal run-offs or flash floods, a great deal of water is suddenly funneled into a narrow, steep-sided canyon. It exits in a burst at Castlegate.

From Kyune to Castlegate, the river falls 1,000 feet in eight miles. Such a fall results in the water reaching Castlegate with tremendous velocity and great quantities. This caused the devastation in 1917.

William Jackson Palmer always claimed that he was the originator of the concept of a narrow gauge railroad when he started and built the original line of the Denver & Rio Grande and the Rio Grande Western. At the time, he placed his rails three feet apart and called them narrow gauge, but there were already many miles of railroad built to gauges less than the standard gauge's 4 feet, $8^1/2$ inches.

He gave many reasons why he originally built from Denver to Salt Lake City-Ogden using narrow gauge: it was more economical to build and maintain; it gave greater balance; and it caused less wear to rolling stock. The only valid reason was the claim for cheaper construction costs and maintenance, but this still was not the true reason.

Palmer built this line as narrow gauge in order to put a lock on the Rocky Mountain Empire and to keep other railroads out of what he considered his private domain. Palmer reasoned that other railroads would

be unable to encroach on him if his railroad was a different gauge. This soon appeared to be an undefendable premise.

By 1887, D&RG accepted that a number of rival railroads were building toward or on its emmpire and all of them were standard gauge. Realizing the disadvantage of transferring lading from narrow gauge to standard gauge, in addition to not participating in transcontinental traffic, they accepted the inevitable. Toward the end of 1887, D&RG started to convert to a three-rail system that would carry both standard and narrow gauge cars between Leadville and Pueblo, Colorado.

This was not successful because of the difference in the heights of standard gauge and narrow gauge rails. Cars leaned and caused many hot boxes. Also, having a different turning radius from two different chords (a straight line intersecting a curve at two points) caused some derailments.

In spring of 1887, David Moffat, the president of the railroad, received approval from the board of directors to standard gauge the main line of the railroad excluding the parts that would eventually become the Narrow Gauge. This would include mileage from Salida to Montrose and Alamosa and from Alamosa to Durango, Santa Fe, Farmington and Silverton. The change was completed by 1890, and the main line was able to enter the battle for transcontinental business.

Turntable at Pueblo, Colorado

In February 1956, I was assigned to Denver as assistant superintendent of the Colorado Division. W.C. (Bill) Horner, who had been with the Rio Grande since the days of the link and pin couplers, was superintendent.

He learned that I was interested in the history of the D&RG, and one day, he brought in an old candy box filled with pictures. These were photographs of incidents and occurrences dating back three or four decades, but unfortunately they were poor quality photographs. One photograph showed an engine partly down in a turntable pit.

Unfortunately, Horner did not have much information on this photograph. He commented that of all the silly and foolish things for a railroad employee to do was to back an engine into the turntable pit.

At the time this photograph was taken, Horner was chief clerk to the superintendent at Pueblo's division office. Horner also said that he had seen two other incidents like this.

When I was chief dispatcher at Alamosa, I went to the turntable to look at our pet engine, the 1000, a C-43, 2-8-0, standard gauge, in the same predicament as Engine No. 1153. This was several years before

Rio Grande Western laid a single track narrow gauge line here and built a wooden bridge over Price River at Castlegate, Utah. The track tied up with the D&RG near the Colorado-Utah state line. *W.H. Jackson, Colorado Historical Society*

This is the same location as in the picture on the previous page, but now the track is double and there is a steel bridge. The line is now part of the D&RGW system, after the RGW and the D&RG merged. The on-coming train is doubleheaded and really smokin' it up! *Colorado Historical Society*

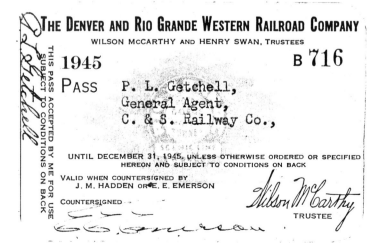

Prior to the Plum Creek flood in 1965 at Denver, the Pueblo Creek flood of 1921 shown here was the greatest railroad damage suffered in one natural disaster by the railroad. This picture was taken June 3, 1921 while cleaning up the ruins in the Pueblo, Colorado yards. *C.E. Rose, Colorado Historical Society*

Horner gave me the photos, and as I looked at Engine No. 1153, it brought back those memories.

At Alamosa, we had one employee almost as much of a pet as Engine No. 1000. Bill Cavaliere was a relief section foreman, and if needed, he worked as a section laborer, switchman, trainman, coal chute operator, machinist helper and a hostler.

But, even the best men can make a mistake occasionally. Working as a hostler, Cavaliere lined the wrong track on the turntable, and, returning to the engine, put it in reverse.

Neither the master mechanic, trainmaster or superintendent had the fortitude to reprimand Cavaliere, and he continued to be Alamosa's pet employee.

Engine #1153 isn't in the best position right now, having run off the track near the turntable after a hostler put the locomotive in reverse instead of forward.

115

Thistle Landslide

The great majority of people give little or no thought to the fact that the physical surface of the Earth is in a constant state of change. In fact, little thought is given to incidents other than those that have occurred in the memory of man—the recorded memory, that is.

Except for geologists and students, most people are prone to think that there has been only minor change and that the surface and appearance of the Earth has remained static since the Precambrian Era (the time between the birth of the planet and the appearance of complex forms of life). The Earth is estimated to be $4^{1}/_{2}$ billion years old, and more than 80 percent of this time falls within this era. Because we measure time in relation to our own life spans, we cannot conceive of the accumulated effect of a constancy of relatively small alterations resulting from cataclysmic changes over the aeons.

Prior to the Cretaceous Period (which started about 135 million years ago and continued for approximately 70 million years) changes to the Earth were more rapid and, therefore, more easily recognizable. Beginning about 65 million years ago the severity of change became less noticeable, and it eventually reached a degree of transformation on a scale only slightly different than the one occurring around us daily somewhere on Earth.

A HEAVY SNOWFALL

In April, 1983—following a winter of heavy snowfall, an accelerated thawing of the snow and above normal rainfall—one of these earthborn occurrences closed the line on the Rio Grande between Thistle and Gomex, Utah. This five miles of railroad runs in the bottom of Spanish Fork Canyon in the Wasatch Range. The physical connection of the railroad was broken for 81 days; during this period the Rio Grande had to move its business by detour over the Union Pacific.

Thistle, until inundated, was located at the confluence of Thistle Creek and the Soldier Fork of the Spanish Fork River. Below this confluence is a very narrow mountain gorge that begins at Thistle and extends to Gomex, a distance of approximately five miles. The sides of the gorge show some exposed rock precipices but, over all, the appearance on both sides is a series of rounded steep slopes running from the summits to the valley. The cover is of grass, forbs and shrubs such as scrub oak, chokecherry, serviceberry and mountain maple. In autumn these hillsides display panoplies of colors beyond imagination.

The slopes of these hillsides border on the natural angle of repose of any loose material such as sand or rock when placed in a pile, usually about 45 degrees. Essentially, the appearance of the hillsides of Spanish Fork Canyon is the same as that of the shores of a lake

A westbound freight passes through Thistle in 1961. *Jim Ozment*

Thistle on April 2, 1983. *Jim Ozment*

when the water level is low and the shores are covered by a growth of vegetation. This is exactly the way the hillsides were formed.

Lake Bonneville was an ancient lake once filled with fresh water. Evidence of its size—about 10 times greater than its remains, the Great Salt Lake—can be seen in the beach deposits high on the mountain sides in the Salt Lake area. Like any large lake, Bonneville had beaches, deltas, sandbars, cliffs and promontories. Its outlet was at Red Rock Pass, Idaho, and it drained into the Snake River. Elevation at this outlet was 7,056 feet (the present elevation). At the peak of Lake Bonneville's capacity the elevation at Thistle was 5,033 feet which indicates that Thistle and the surrounding area were under about 2,000 feet of water. When the lake finally began to evaporate, the receding waters left behind beach deposits far up the mountains (once the shores of the lake) around Thistle. Eventually, this was covered with vegetation and soil.

This residual overburden lays on the impervious rock of a synclinal fold. Spanish Fork River's course is east to west in the trough of this fold. The main tributaries of the Spanish Fork River are Soldier Fork, which heads near Soldier Summit at an elevation of 7,440 feet, and Thistle Creek at Hilltop on the Marysvale Branch at an elevation of 6,435 feet. These tributaries and their small feeders drain an area measuring about 50 miles north-south and 30 miles east-west. The greater part of this drainage lacks heavy foliage and is predominantly covered only by light foliage or scant grass. There is much exposed shale, rock, sand and hardpan soil. Run off is rapid. Soldier Fork falls 2,400 feet in 30 miles, and Thistle Creek falls 1,402 feet in 23 miles.

APRIL 13, 1983

All of these factors contributed to the events of April 13, 1983. A heavy, ancient beach deposit laying on a section of rock in a mini-valley on the north side of

An aerial view just west of Thistle, showing how the water has wiped out much of the trackage in the area. Service was suspended on April 14—this view was taken April 26. *Jim Ozment*

Spanish Fork River became saturated down to the rock. Cohesion was lost, and the mass—eventually estimated as containing three million cubic yards—turned loose. Gravity carried it to the bottom of the gorge where it formed a dam which completely filled the void and measured 200 feet high. As the mass settled, still saturated, it came to rest at the natural angle of repose and formed a watertight dam almost resembling a carefully constructed Earth fill dam.

The runoff from the drainage area could not be diverted, and it continued to flow down its normal course. A lake began to form, and it soon became apparent that the dam would continue to retain this flow and inundate the entire gorge until the flow decreased or an overflow at the dam could be constructed. To prevent a large accumulation of debris against the dam, property owners, the state of Utah and the Rio Grande began to remove buildings, struc-

Water continued to pour into Spanish Fork Canyon behind the landslide dam. *Jim Ozment*

Barge with super volume pumps help lower the lake level; taken in May, 1983. *Jim Ozment*

Debris is everywhere on the margins of the lake as the water level was lowered. *Jim Ozment*

tures and any other salvageable material ahead of the rising water.

On April 14, 1983 the Rio Grande suspended train movement. An engineering decision had been reached that there were no alternatives: A line change would be necessary to restore service. This line change would require a tunnel with an east portal above the anticipated high water level and a west portal safely beyond the dam and impounded water.

In the meantime, the state of Utah, fearing the dam might rupture and cause damage lower downstream, began operations to minimize this possibility. At this stage, an overflow was not the answer. Huge pumps were brought in and installed on a barge on the lake. The flow was controlled, and the lake level was lowered some. Preparations were also started to re-route Highway No. 6 higher up on the hillside.

Only a full-length book could do justice to the boring of the tunnel—approximately 3,000 feet in length— the construction of the necessary line change and the building of the new segment of Highway No. 6. At 3:12 p.m. on July 4, 1983 Denver & Rio Grande Western Engine No. 3107, coupled with four other units, pulled a long eastbound freight through the new tunnel. At this time, automobiles also were moving on the new highway.

All in all, both the railroad and the highway ultimately benefited from the Thistle landslide. Unfortunately, the Marysvale Branch of the Rio Grande will never operate again.

This was the construction camp set up for tunnel. *Jim Ozment*

RIGHT. West end of the new tunnel with view of part of the new line, State Highway #6 and a segment of the drainage pipes. *Jim Ozment*

BELOW. At 3:12 p.m. on July 4, 1983 the first D&RGW freight train rolled over the new line and through the tunnel. *Jim Ozment*

Engine #273 hauls a one-car sightseeing special train for some of Palmer's friends over Marshall Pass. *W.H. Jackson, Colorado Historical Society*

Chapter 5
Passenger, Presidential, Troop and Special Trains

Palmer Specials

General William Jackson Palmer retired as president of the Denver & Rio Grande on August 9, 1883 because of severe criticism by Eastern stockholders and bondholders of his policies and management.

For at least two years prior to retirement, he drove himself and all who were associated with him toward higher accomplishments. With an engine and business car standing ready at all times, he along with associates, friends and financiers, traveled back and forth

The *Yampa Valley Mail,* with Engine #801, approaches Gore Canyon on April 1, 1950. *M.D. McCarther collection*

over the newly built D&RG lines. William H. Jackson often accompanied these "Palmer Specials" or was working nearby and photographed these excursions for the archives or publicity. Every time Palmer had an engine with his car out on the line, it was operated as a "Special." Only much later did the word "Special" come to be used by the U.S. rail fraternity to indicate a very special train was being run.

Jackson took this photograph on Marshall Pass, either in the fall of 1882 or spring of 1883. Engine No. 273, a 2-8-0, was built in February 1882. Palmer resigned on August 9, 1883, and thereafter, had no rights or authority to order or run these "Specials." Of course, he could do so on his own railroad, the Rio Grande Western in Utah, but he lost his clout on the D&RG.

The *Yampa Valley Mail* at Kremmling, Colorado in 1950. *M.D. McCarter collection*

Yampa Valley Mail

During the days the Moffat Line operated, the town of Craig and all other communities between Craig, Colorado and Denver were the lifeblood of the Moffat Line. The Rio Grande tended to downgrade this.

On January 1, 1951 the daytime locals and the former, tri-weekly nighttime Moffat Road trains were dropped. In lieu of these, air-conditioned coaches and a 12-section, one drawing room sleeper was run daily as part of the consist of *Mountaineer* trains Nos. 19 and 20 between Denver and Bond, Colorado. At this diverging point to Craig, the Yampa Valley portion was cut off and handled to and from Craig as a separate train.

The people in the towns along the line objected to the elimination of the daytime service. On September 5, 1954 the outcries resulted in daylight service re-established with train Nos. 9 and 10. The trains were given the name of *Yampa Valley Mail*.

Timetables of November 1963 retained trains No. 9 and No. 10, but changed the name to *Yampa Valley*. The overall decline in passengers continued, and the Rio Grande abandoned a number of passenger trains during the next five years. On April 7, 1968 the *Yampa Mail,* the last passenger service to Yampa Valley and northwestern Colorado, was also abandoned.

I felt the loss of this service as much as those who lived along the line. In 1956, I was transferred to Denver where I spent the final 20 years of my Rio Grande service (except for a temporary assignment at Salt Lake City). I frequently rode the *Yampa Mail* on various assignments, and I enjoyed the roundtrip from Denver to Craig and the overnight stay more than riding on the *California Zephyr.*

Shooting the breeze with crew members and passengers was like riding the old Narrow Gauge *San Juan* passenger trains between Alamosa and Durango. It is no wonder that the people of northwestern Colorado resented the Rio Grande taking away one of their special loves and traditions.

The Silver Vista

The Silver Vista was built in the Rio Grande shops at Burnham, Colorado, in 1947 from work coach car No. 0313 in order to answer the growing demand for a car to be used on excursions, but specifically for assignment to the Silverton Branch where railfan interest was tremendous. The car was very popular, but unfortunately after six years of success, it burned in a fire at the Alamosa car shops in 1953. A replacement was never built.

The Silver Vista was designed in the MP&CD department (Motive Power and Car Department), and one of the draftsmen put all the ideas together in what could be called a manufacturer's plate. Essentially, its

The ultimate in a railfan sightseeing car, the *Silver Vista,* #313, was burned in a shop fire at Alamosa. It was built specifically for service on the Silverton Branch in 1947. *Colorado Historical Society*

W.H. Jackson took this picture of a chartered sightseeing trip through the Black Canyon. *Colorado Historical Society*

Sightseeing car #780 ready to leave Glenwood Springs eastward. *Colorado Historical Society*

design was derived from the vista dome cars to be used on the *California Zephyr.*

The comfortable seats were enclosed and protected from the weather and flying cinders, and the car's modern appearance produced a sightseeing railcar much different from the three built as narrow gauge open cars and put into service about 1904, the year they first appeared in the equipment portion of the D&RG's roster. They were discontinued in about 1923, the last year found listed in the roster.

These cars were as follows: No. 500, Royal Gorge; No. 501, Black Canyon; and, No. 502, Argus. The Royal Gorge seated 48 passengers; the other two each seated 52 passengers. They were approximately 36 feet long, 8 feet wide and had a total above-the-rail height of 6 feet. Mounted on archbar trucks, they were not nearly as smooth riding as the Silver Vista.

The Silver Vista was so well-built that it never presented its crew with any troubles. From accounts received from crew members and supervisors who did ride the Silver Vista, the same could not be said about its passengers. It was never an extra fare car and was seated on a first-come, first-served basis. Those who were lucky enough to get a seat early during the trip were reluctant to let others share this comfortable seating. Trainmen tried to preserve a modicum of tranquility, but they were limited by company rules against altercations.

I have always regretted that I never rode on a train that had the Silver Vista in its consist. I was promoted to chief dispatcher at Alamosa in October 1947 after the tourist season was over and the Silver Vista was placed in storage. This job kept me office-bound until 1950 when I was appointed trainmaster on the Alamosa division. I stayed on this assignment until June 1953 when I was transferred to the Salt Lake Division. As trainmaster at Alamosa, I had opportunities to ride the Silver Vista, but for one reason or another, I never did. In the all of 1953, I received information that it burned. There went my chance of riding this well-built car.

The *Prospector*

Nationally and internationally, the *California Zephyr* was the most popular train operating on the Rio Grande tracks, but for everyday use and convenience, the *Prospector* ran a very close second in popularity to the *Zephyr.* The *Zephyr* was a glamour girl; the *Prospector* was a hardworking haus frau.

The *Prospector* was introduced with train schedule numbers Nos. 7 and 8. Service began on November 17, 1941, and the train was a stainless steel, streamlined, overnight train that ran between Denver, Salt Lake City and Ogden via Moffat Tunnel.

The *Prospector* consisted of two trains, each powered by four 192 hp diesel engines with six cylinders per engine, and each train had two cars. On one train, the cars were named John Evans and David Moffat, after renowned Colorado pioneers. The cars on the other train were named after Brigham Young and Hebert C. Kimball, Utah pioneers and Mormon leaders.

The front car had a luggage compartment, a 44-passenger coach section, and "his" and "hers" lavatories. The rear car had eight standard Pullman sections, two "chambrettes" (small sleeping chambers), a dinette-observation section and two segregated men's and women's rooms.

These Budd cars, although popular with the public, were a source of never-ending trouble. Breakdowns not only delayed their schedules, but contributed frequently to the delays of other trains. It became almost a rule that a 700 or 800 Class engine was on standby to aid a crippled Budd car train. Frequently, it was necessary to hold a freight train in a terminal and use its engine to forward either Train No. 7 or No. 8. The use of Budd cars was discontinued at the end of July 1942.

REVIVAL

On October 14, 1945 World War II ended, and the name *Prospector* as the name of a train was revived. As re-established, Trains Nos. 7 and 8 were used for morning arrivals and late afternoon departures at Denver and Salt Lake City. The consist included a chair car, diner, tourist and standard sleeping cars, and one of the "Canon" (Canyon) series lounge/observation cars. Originally steam-powered, in 1946 it was described as "diesel-powered." Another change came in February 1947 with the discontinuation of the lounge/observation cars in the consists. In their place, the trains carried one of the "Mount" series diner-lounge car.

On May 30, 1948 Trains Nos. 7 and 8 had, in addition to the designation "diesel-powered," the word "streamlined." The inauguration of the *California Zephyr* made this old, heavyweight equipment on these trains look dowdy and not in keeping with the image of a progressive railroad. Using some of the 25 streamlined cars obtained from the Chesapeake & Ohio, in addition to three others that were bought from the C&O near the end of 1949, Trains Nos. 7 and 8 were fully streamlined.

REDUCING MILEAGE

Early in 1950, a nationwide strike by coal miners began. The Interstate Commerce Commission ordered all railroads to reduce train mileage even though individual railroads were dieselized. The Rio Grande consolidated Royal Gorge route trains, which originated at Pueblo, Colorado. The consolidation worked

Eastbound *Prospector,* Train #8, is on the "Big Ten" curve approaching Rocky. Engine #5574 leads a second helper diesel. *Bill Warren, Denver Public Library, Western History Section*

well and was without adverse effects. When the strike was over, the consolidation was permanent.

New stainless steel cars continued to be built during the spring, summer and fall of 1950. Some were immediately placed in *Prospector* service so that a new timetable dated July 1, 1950 carried a full-color illustration of the fast, overnight trains.

The *Prospector* was discontinued on May 28, 1967. In many respects, its loss was more poignant than that of the *California Zephyr.* The *California Zephyr* had more polish, more sophistication and always gave its passengers that little extra touch of service and de rigueur. Hollywood starlets and prominent

people traveled on the *Zephyr's* route, and it came close to being guilty of exhibitionism.

Personally, I preferred the *Prospector.* Boarding at either Denver or Salt Lake City, a passenger could enjoy an excellent dinner and then spend the evening with substantial people of the Rocky Mountain Empire: stockmen, businessmen and businesswomen, and down-to-earth people who were pleasant company. Then you could go to bed for a fine night's sleep and arrive at your destination ready for a day's work. There were many people who felt the same way about the *Prospector,* and, when its service was discontinued, it was sorely missed.

Presidential Special at Pueblo, Colorado

The Rio Grande, along with other railroads, operated only two special "Specials." One was run on demand, and, if the price was right, it was dubbed a "Silk Special," rushing newly arrived silk from the Orient to Eastern markets. The other was organized and operated on a gold-plated basis for "POTAMUS," the Morse telegrapher's Phillips code for "President Of The United States Of America."

Today, the term "Special Train" is usually interpreted incorrectly. Many times in order to obtain a trainload shipment of a commodity or a group going to some convention, passenger and freight traffic representatives would assure potential clients that their trains would be run as a "Special." Advertising and publicity might carry this banner, but unless a directive came down from upper management, the train received good service and handling, but not to the degree that other business and trains would receive delays.

PREPARATION BEGINS

A *Presidential Special* was different. Organizing and running a train for the most important person in the country was quite different from preparing a helicopter or Air Force One today with only a few hours notice.

Ordinarily, it required about two weeks lead time to arrange for the operation of a *Presidential Special*. After the President announced his desires, a group of government transportation officials began contacting railroad managements about the lines that would be involved. They announced the destination, date and tentative schedule; however, they never divulged the reason for the trip. That was the President's business.

With other pertinent details ironed out, each railroad went into action. The pending trip's itinerary was released to the press without any indication as to why the train was being run. This itinerary allowed local communities to inform their citizens that they could have an opportunity to see and sometimes hear the most important person in the country. Usually, only one representative from each of the two major news associations, Associated Press and United Press International, were allowed to ride the President's train. Many people came to see and hear the President at wayside stops.

From experience, the railroads knew the minimum requirements for operating the *Presidential Special* and the security measures that had to be taken. Then, each railroad began "gold-plating" equipment and service to secure future presidential business.

Each railroad selected one or more engines as deemed necessary and gave them a thorough mechan-

ical fitness inspection, including a polishing job that left them looking like new.

While this was being done, each of the railroad operating departments was involved. Station grounds and the right-of-way underwent cleanup operations. Train dispatchers were instructed about schedules and procedures for assuring a safe margin of time on each

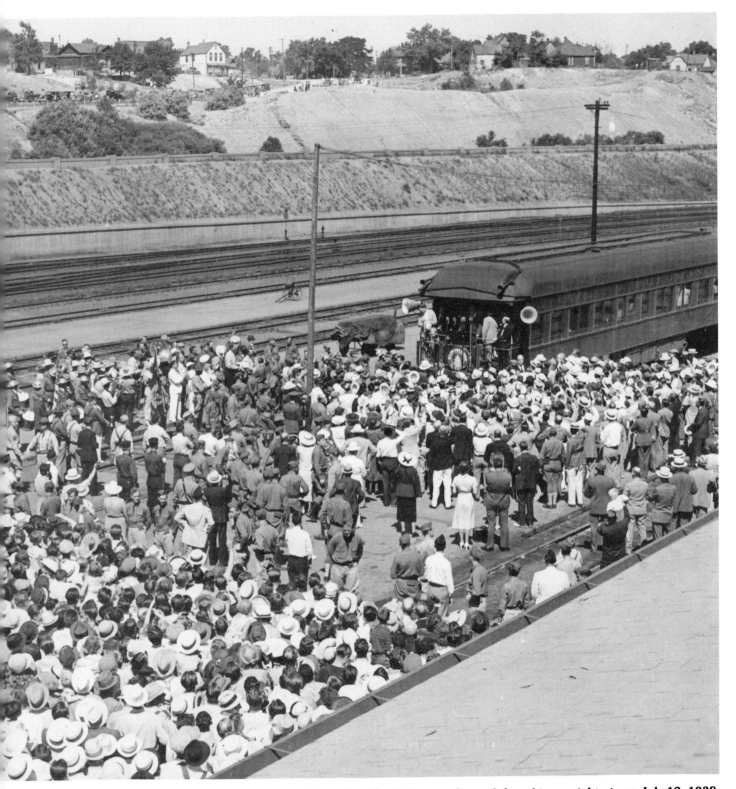

Pueblo residents turned out in droves to see and hear Franklin D. Roosevelt speak from his special train on July 12, 1938.

segment of track as the *Presidential Special* advanced. A pilot train ran ahead of the *Presidential Special* as an extra precaution against any track failure or other mishap.

Crews for the engine, train, dining car and Pullmans were selected and assigned, and their responsibilities were reviewed. These assignments bypassed normal seniority or first-in, first-out working agreements in order to have only the most competent and acceptable employees on the train. Road foremen of equipment, then called traveling engineers or traveling "hogheads," and trainmasters were assigned. In addition, the division superintendent, dining car supervisor and a Pullman supervisor were chosen. To insure

Roosevelt's special train, going through to the coast, was met by many people in 1938.

against electrical, plumbing, heating or air-conditioning problems, qualified men rode the train to make prompt repairs, if necessary. These and other details were considered the minimum needed to "gold-plate" the train's successful and safe operation.

THE BIG DAY

On the big day, communities where stops were scheduled were kept informed of the President's arrival times. Crowds gathered in advance, such as the one in the photograph at Pueblo on July 12, 1938. This crowd was larger than usual, and they did not know why President Franklin D. Roosevelt was stopping briefly in their town, neither did they care. At this time, FDR reached the pinnacle of his popularity and enjoyed almost god-like status.

Inaugurated for his second term in 1937, FDR was credited with bringing the country out of the Depression, with the establishment of Social Security, stable banks, the Railroad Retirement Act and many more social improvements. He was also active in developing trade agreements with Canada and other countries and establishing the basis for an updated, more realistic Monroe Doctrine in the Americas. In 1938, he was especially active and rode the *Presidential Special* frequently.

During this time, Adolf Hitler was taking over Europe, and Japan was on the offensive with China, so it was necessary for him to frequently travel around the country to calm citizens' fears. When a *Presidential Special* with FDR on board was nearby, the citizens gathered to hear this great man should he speak.

Troop Trains

World War II and its heavy movement of troops by rail gave the Rio Grande an opportunity to demonstrate what an outstanding railroad it was. No one will ever know how many troop or impedimenta trains carrying equipment and supplies moved over its line. In 1945, a record of the number of troop trains hauled was kept, but it did not include the impedimenta trains. In that year, 2,395 troop trains were hauled.

There were only a few short segments of centralized traffic control on the Rio Grande during this period. It was necessary to establish many new train order offices since trains were moved and governed by train orders. Western Union, postal telegraph, press houses and brokerage houses had many trained telegraphers, so as a result, we hired them and gave them a few days of training and a certificate for passing the Book of Rules examination.

As scarce as Morse telegraphers were, telephone equipment was even harder to find. What equipment we did receive was installed in less isolated locations, and women telephone operators were assigned to these locations.

Train dispatchers were on a permanent draft-deferment regardless of their age, health or marital status. Though not at the front lines, all dispatchers sweated and toiled through the entire war. We were not alone. Train, engine service, mechanical and maintenance employees all worked long hours under gruelling conditions. Rio Grande workers were no worse off than those who worked on other war lines, however.

It was with a great deal of trepidation that dispatchers learned of the many non-railroad telegraphers with whom we would be working. Fortunately, these people learned very quickly and became bona fide railroaders that we could depend upon. It was a marvel the way a little slip of a girl or a woman with gray showing in her hair, on a dark night, could stand at train order hoop distance from trackside clearance and hand up orders to a crew member in the big Mallet as it thundered past.

GRAND JUNCTION

Train dispatching at Pueblo, Salida and Salt Lake City was rough, but the one that separated the men from the boys was at Grand Junction, either the east or west end. If a dispatcher did not issue at least 100 train orders during an eight-hour shift there, he had an easy trick. The orders were just part of it. There were clearance cards to issue, train and engine crew boards to enter on the train sheets and "OS" reports (Morse telegrapher code to alert dispatcher that a train report is to be made) to keep current and miscellaneous data to enter.

The Grand Junction train sheets, which were six feet long, could carry 50 trains on each side of the station column. Usually, we spliced on more columns by 5:00 p.m. or 6:00 p.m. each evening. Fresh train sheets were started at 12:01 a.m. daily.

WHO'S IN CHARGE

During the first year of troop movements, the U.S. Armed Forces officer in command of a train was omnipotent in respect to the movement of his train. Unfortunately, few, if any, of these train commanders had any knowledge about railroading.

One night when I was working a second trick, a troop train arrived at Bond, Colorado on the Moffat route with flat wheels on its kitchen car. The car inspector said that it needed a rewheeling job, a two-or three-hour delay. The train commander instructed that the train keep moving. One thing led to another until the train commander and the reigning railroad supervisor on duty at Grand Junction had it out. The U.S. Army won, and I was instructed to clear the train with orders to run at reduced speed.

As naive as I was at the time, I knew that flat wheels nicked rails, and nicked rails broke. Remonstrating got me nowhere. The train proceeded, and the flat wheels did nick the rails. In the days that followed, many were replaced. The flat-wheeled train arrived at Grand Junc-

A 22-car troop train bears down the Arkansas River Valley behind a 4-6-6-4 with Engine #3733; the train is about to disturb the ghosts of the old South Park where it used to cross the Rio Grande. The old DSP&P roadbed is in the foreground. *Philip R. Hastings, Denver Public Library, Western History Section*

The *California Zephyr* passes through some of America's most scenic country. Here it's at American Fork, Utah, with the Oquirrh Mountains as a backdrop. *D&RGW Railroad*

tion about 8:00 a.m. where its wheels were replaced. I was there to see it hobble into the station. When the superintendent arrived at his office and checked for the morning's problems, he learned of the incident with the kitchen car. He called me into his office and chewed me out for not having the guts to stand up for what I knew was right, even if my opponent was the U.S. Army.

Dispatchers, even not so brave ones were scarce, so I was not fired. The night supervisor kept his job, too, after he received a verbal lashing.

OTHER SERVICE

The Korean War put the Rio Grande and some other railroads back into the business of carrying troops, although the movement was not as heavy as during World War II. Starting in June 1950, the Rio

Grande was far from dieselization, and the troop trains were almost totally steam-powered. A truce was declared in July 1951, and a peace agreement was signed on July 27, 1953.

Prior to this signing, many of the battle-worn troops returned to the United States. The picture of the troop train taken in 1952 near Nathrop was probably carrying some of these men. When dieselization was complete, the water tank at Nathrop was dismantled, and, a few years later, the stockyards also were dismantled. The Rio Grande was no longer in the troop-carrying business.

The *California Zephyr*

In Europe, the most famed passenger train was the *Orient Express,* but even at its glorious best, it could not hold a candle to the *California Zephyr.*

In 1945, the Rio Grande passenger timetables announced that there soon would be a group of six stainless steel trains running between Chicago and San Francisco that would provide a train each day out of Chicago and San Francisco. The trains would be known as the *California Zephyrs* and have vista dome observation cars. I attribute the design of the vista dome cars to the car builder Budd, but in Robert G. Athearn's *Rebel of the Rockies,* he states that in 1944, the idea for the vista domes was the brainchild of Cyrus R. Osborn, general manager and vice president of General Motors.

I still think that Budd designed the vista domes because he frequently rode the headend of the Budd cars trying to improve their performance and often talked about designing observation cars with roof windows. Also by 1944, designs for the *California Zephyr* incorporating the vista domes were already on the drafting boards.

THE ALCOS

Awaiting the final inauguration of the *California Zephyr,* the Rio Grande used Alco locomotives Nos. 600 and 601, two three-unit engines with 6,000 hp, ordered specifically for use on the *Zephyr* trains, and they were received ahead of the vista dome cars.

The delivery of the cars for the *Zephyr's* consist were delayed. A few cars appeared during February, March and April of 1948, but since delivery was sporadic, they were used on the *Exposition Flyer.* Eventually, the Rio Grande had a train of 11 cars. It used Alco Engine No. 601 to operate a special break-in

An Alco pulling the *Zephyr* eastward exits the Moffat Tunnel at East Portal. *Colorado Historical Society*

demonstration from Denver to Salt Lake City on March 15, 1949. The train returned from Salt Lake City the following day.

The Alcos did have a few faults. Unlike the EMD F series, they did not tick like a finely tuned watch. They leaked oil and required more maintenance than an EMD. For railroads that had both EMDs and Alcos to maintain, it soon became apparent it was best to have only one locomotive supplier. Denver was far from the source of repair parts, and, as a result, the store department kept buying parts in anticipation of future repairs. Many of these parts were never needed, and, eventually, the inventories began to show that money was wasted on unneeded parts.

An economy-minded railroad cannot afford locomotives built by two manufacturers, not if the repair parts are not interchangeable. The Rio Grande had many more EMDs than Alcos, so some Alco units were sold.

Alcos had a place on high-speed passenger trains, but they were not designed for the heavy tonnage freight drags on the Rio Grande's grades. Their specifications were impressive:

SERVICE ENGINES	PASSENGER ENGINES
Class	DE3(AIA-AIA)
Builder	American Locomotive Company
Wheel Diameter	40 inches
Rail load	613,320 pounds
Tractive effort	147,792 pounds (This kept them from being freight haulers.)
Engine hp rating	6,000
Cylinders	16
Bore and stroke	9 x 10$\frac{1}{2}$ inches
Fuel Capacity	3,600 gallons (Refueling was not required on *Zephyr's* runs.)

Unit 6002 was converted to a steam-generator car No. 253 in October 1965. Unit 6012 already was converted to steam-generator No. 252 in July 1965. Units 6001 and 6013 came with steam generators for passenger use. On June 20, 1967, units 6001, 6011 and 6013 were sold to Precision Engineering.

SMOOTH SAILING

For those privileged few who were permitted to ride the cab of an Alco engine, the ride was smooth. It was a treat to board the engine cab at Denver with a 1,000 mile lunch and a thermos of coffee and stay there until you arrived at Salt Lake City. The journey over the mountains on a sunny morning when the hoarfrost

was on the spruce trees and deer and elk were feeding in open places was a never-ending delight. The journey through Glenwood Canyon and Ruby Canyon then across the desert offered other spectacular vistas.

Glenwood Springs, Colorado has long been touted as a place where the water of the hot springs is both soothing and curative. Unlike the residents of many quasi-rural or tourist towns, the populace did not rush to the depot when the train arrived, especially during the winter.

Unlike Aspen, Glenwood Springs did not have many colorful characters in its town, but there were a few. One character lived alone in a small dwelling he built in a nook of Glenwood Canyon. Because he never told anyone his name or background, he was dubbed "Hermit of Glenwood Canyon." He really was not a true hermit since he fraternized with the people of Glenwood, and he was garrulous to the point of being a nuisance.

Passengers looking out of the vista dome on the *Zephyr* thought this hermit — the Hermit of Glenwood Canyon — was a real thrill to watch. *Colorado Historical Society*

When he was in town, he visited the depot to watch the *California Zephyr's* comings and goings. His beard, pipe, crumpled hat and boots—his entire appearance—appeared to be an assumed identity. Though his appearance did not indicate his knowledge, he spoke like a well-read, widely traveled and well-educated man.

During the 1960s when the weather became cold, he battened down his cabin and disappeared until the return of spring. He never revealed where he went or what he did. He always paid for goods in cash, though no one knew his source of income.

Travelers on the *California Zephyr* always noticed him and asked who he was. Perhaps, he made money from these camera-toting tourists eager to capture the local color.

Car *Silver Sky* of the *California Zephyr* was a luxury car. A portable set of steps was available at Glenwood to place for passengers who wished to use them. Rear cars of the *Zephyrs* did not have vestibules. Up to March 21, 1959, after a decade of service, 1.5 million passengers had been carried; daily occupancy hit 89.4 percent. *Colorado Historical Society*

The westbound *California Zephyr* at
Glenwood Springs, Colorado in its hey-
day. Judging from the automobiles, this
picture may have been taken soon after
World War II. Note the two Alco PA-
style diesel locomotives on the headend, the four dome cars up front and the
rear end single dome car. *Colorado
Historical Society*

DENVER & RIO GRANDE RAILROAD.

EMPLOYES' TIME-TABLE

No. 16.

TO TAKE EFFECT 12.01 A. M. NOV. 9TH, 1890.

STANDARD TIME, 105th MERIDIAN.

THIS TIME-TABLE is for the guidance of employes only, and is not intended for the information of the public, or as an advertisement of any train. The Company reserves the right to vary from it at pleasure.

THIRD DIVISION—Salida and Gunnison—FIRST DISTRICT.

TIME-TABLE 16 — Nov. 9, 1890.

EASTWARD

Station (and sidings)	Miles from Gunnison	2 Atlantic Express (Arrive Daily A.M.)	4 Oregon and Salt Lake Express (Arrive Daily P.M.)	304 Durango and Denver Express (Arrive Daily P.M.)	66 California Fast Freight (Arrive Daily P.M.)	364 Denver Mixed (Arrive Daily Exc. Sunday P.M.)	374 Durango and Denver Freight (Arrive Daily Exc. Sunday P.M.)	342 Local Freight (Arrive Daily P.M.)	372 Orient Freight (Arrive Daily Exc. Sunday P.M.)
SALIDA (s, N) 5.0	78.8	11.15 / 10.55	10.20 / 10.05	10.20 / 9.55	4.40	4.00	4.30	7.15	6.35
PONCHA JUNC. Pn (D) 4.5	68.8	10.40	9.53	9.42	4.20	3.42	4.12	6.54	6.13
OTTO 1.4	64.3	10.22	9.34	9.21	3.51		3.44	6.26	5.44
MEARS JUNC. Mr (D) 2.4	62.9	10.16	9.27	9.15	3.43		3.35	6.17	5.35
SHIRLEY 3.6	60.5	10.07	9.18		3.30			6.03	
KEENE 2.2	56.9	9.53	9.02		3.08			5.40	
GRAY'S Gy (D) 3.4	54.7	9.45	8.53		2.54			5.28	
POCONO 3.2	51.3	9.30	8.37		2.32			5.06	
MARSHALL PASS Mp (N) 4.2	48.1	9.17 / 9.12	8.22 / 8.15		2.10 / 2.00			4.45 / 4.35	
SHAWANO 3.7	43.9	8.57	7.57		1.30			4.06	
CHESTER (D) 4.4	40.2	8.35	7.42		1.04			3.42	
BUXTON 4.4	35.8	8.09	7.26		12.37			3.15	
SARGENT Sg (N) 4.8	31.4	7.55 / 7.50	7.12 / 6.52		12.20 / 11.56			2.55 / 2.20	
ELKO 3.5	26.6	7.40	6.41		11.37			2.00	
CROOKTON 3.9	23.1	7.32	6.34		11.23			1.44	
DOYLE 1.0	19.2	7.24	6.26		11.07			1.27	
BONITA 6.4	18.2	7.22	6.24		11.03			1.23	
PARLIN Pa (D) 5.3	11.8	7.09	6.10		10.37			12.54	
MOUNDS 6.5	6.5	6.59	5.59		10.10			12.32	
GUNNISON Gu (N)		6.45 / 6.25	5.45 / 5.37		9.45 / 9.00			12.05	
Leave Daily (times)		(4.10)	(4.20)	(.40)	(6.55)	(.18)	(.55)	(7.10)	(1.00)

WESTWARD

Station (and sidings)	Miles from Denver	303 Denver and Durango Express (Leave Daily A.M.)	3 Salt Lake and Oregon Express (Leave Daily A.M.)	1 Pacific Coast Express (Leave Daily P.M.)	65 California Fast Freight (Leave Daily A.M.)	363 Monarch Mixed (Leave Daily Exc. Sunday A.M.)	373 Alamosa and Durango Freight (Leave Daily Exc. Sunday A.M.)	341 Local Freight (Leave Daily A.M.)	371 Orient Freight (Leave Daily Exc. Sunday A.M.)
SALIDA (s, N) 5.0	216.5	6.30 / 6.55	6.30 / 7.00	8.15 / 8.40	9.05	8.50	8.40	6.20	10.55
PONCHA JUNC. Pn (D) 4.5	221.5	7.07	7.13	6.54	9.23	9.10	9.00	6.40	11.10
OTTO 1.4	226.0	7.25	7.30	7.12	10.02		9.26	7.15	11.38
MEARS JUNC. Mr (D) 2.4	227.4	7.31	7.36	7.18	10.16		9.35	7.26	11.46
SHIRLEY 3.6	229.8		7.45	7.27	10.30			7.45 / 7.50	
KEENE 2.2	233.4		8.00	7.42	10.57			8.10	
GRAY'S Gy (D) 3.4	235.6		8.08	7.50	11.12			8.24	
POCONO 3.2	239.0		8.22	8.05	11.36			8.49	
MARSHALL PASS Mp (N) 4.2	242.2		8.35 / 8.40	8.20 / 8.30	12.00 / 12.10			9.12 / 9.22	
SHAWANO 3.7	246.4		8.57	8.48	12.38			9.54	
CHESTER (D) 4.4	250.1		9.15	9.07	1.04			10.18	
BUXTON 4.4	254.5		9.36	9.27	1.30			10.47	
SARGENT Sg (N) 4.8	258.9		9.50 / 9.56	9.40 / 9.45	2.26 / 2.26			12.07 / 12.07	
ELKO 3.5	263.7		10.05	9.57	2.42			12.33	
CROOKTON 3.9	267.2		10.18	10.05	2.56			12.52	
DOYLE 1.0	271.1		10.22	10.14	3.10			1.14	
BONITA 6.4	272.1		10.24	10.18	3.14			1.23	
PARLIN Pa (D) 5.3	278.5		10.37	10.31	3.37			1.50	
MOUNDS 6.5	283.8		10.50	10.43	3.55			2.13	
GUNNISON Gu (N)	290.3		11.05 / 11.25	10.58 / 11.08	4.20 / 4.55			2.40	
Arrive (times)	(73.8)	(.36)	(4.05)	(4.18)	(7.15)	(.29)	(.55)	(8.20)	(.31)

No train shall leave Salida, Marshall Pass, Sargent or Gunnison without special order or clearance ticket.

Third District Trains must not leave Mears Junction, nor 364 leave Poncha Junction without special order or clearance ticket.

Water Tank 7. 2 miles east of Buxton.

THIRD DIVISION—Gunnison and Grand Junction—SECOND DISTRICT.

WESTWARD — TIME-TABLE 16, Nov. 9, 1890. — EASTWARD

Third Class 351 Local Freight (Leave Daily A.M.)	Second Class 333 Lake City Mixed (Leave Daily Exc. Sunday P.M.)	Second Class 65 California Fast Freight (Leave Daily P.M.)	First Class 3 Salt Lake and Oregon Express (Leave Daily A.M.)	First Class 1 Pacific Coast Express (Leave Daily P.M.)	MILES FROM DENVER	STATIONS AND SIDINGS	MILES FROM GRAND JUNCTION	First Class 2 Atlantic Express (Arrive Daily A.M.)	First Class 4 Oregon and Salt Lake Express (Arrive Daily)	Second Class 66 California Fast Freight (Arrive Daily A.M.)	Second Class 334 Denver Mixed (Arrive Daily Exc. Sunday P.M.)	Third Class 352 Local Freight (Arrive Daily P.M.)	CAR CAPACITY OF SIDINGS, LOCATION OF SCALES, WATER, FUEL AND TURNING STATIONS
7.20		4.20 / 4.55	11.05 / 11.25	10.58 / 11.08	290.3	N GUNNISON (Gu)	134.9	6.45 / 6.25	5.45 / 5.37	9.45 / 9.00		9.05	● O Y § X 363
					291.3	D., S.P. & P. CROSSING No. 3	133.9						
7.40		5.13	11.37	11.23	295.4	ABERDEEN JUNC.	129.8	6.12	5.24	8.40		8.40	48
7.44		5.22	11.39	11.25	296.2	HIERRO	129.0	6.10	5.22	8.36		8.36	29
8.12		5.46	11.54	11.41	301.7	D KEZAR (Kz)	123.5	5.56	5.09	8.12		8.10	46
8.45		6.15	12.12	12.01	308.8	□ CEBOLLA (La)	116.4	5.38	4.52	7.44		7.37	○
9.20 / 9.25	4.39	6.44	12.30	12.21	315.7	N SAPINERO (Sa)	109.5	5.20	4.34	7.15 / 7.00	12.15	7.04 / 6.38	O Y 157
9.32	4.44	6.50	12.35	12.26	316.4	LAKE JUNC.	108.8	5.15	4.29	6.55	12.10	6.32	
10.00		7.15	12.54	12.48	322.5	CURECANTI (Cn)	102.7	4.57	4.10	6.30		6.06	31
10.30		7.42	1.15	1.12	329.2	CRYSTAL CREEK	96.0	4.37	3.50	6.02		5.38	14
10.37 / 10.52		7.50 / 8.10	1.20 / 1.25	1.19 / 1.24	330.6	N CIMARRON (Rn)	94.6	4.32 / 4.27	3.45 / 3.25	5.55 / 5.45		5.30 / 5.15	● O Y 108
11.33 / 11.47		8.55 / 9.00	1.54	1.55	336.3	D CERRO SUMMIT (Cr)	88.9	3.59	2.56	5.10 / 5.05		4.35 / 4.22	Y 19
12.27		9.45	2.25	2.28	342.9	D CEDAR CREEK (Dr)	82.3	3.30	2.25	4.50		3.40	O Y 42
12.46		10.08	2.42	2.43	348.0	FAIRVIEW	77.2	3.15	2.10	3.56		3.20	47
1.05 / 1.55		10.25 / 10.35	3.00 / 3.16	2.58 / 3.08	353.2	N MONTROSE (Ms)	72.0	3.00 / 2.54	1.55 / 1.40	3.30 / 3.08		3.00 / 1.55	● O Y 248
2.20		10.57	3.30	3.22	359.0	MENOKEN	66.2	2.38	1.23	2.43 / 2.38		1.30	43
2.40		11.15	3.42	3.34	364.0	COLOROW	61.2	2.15	1.08	2.10		1.13 / 1.08	○ 38
3.02		11.36	3.55	3.46	369.1	CHIPETA	56.1	2.13	12.53	1.42		12.46	44
3.25		11.59	4.09	4.00	374.4	N DELTA (Dt)	50.8	2.00	12.36	1.10		12.23	O Y 75
3.44		12.19	4.21	4.12	379.1	ROUBIDEAU	46.1	1.48	12.22	12.44		12.04	42
3.55		12.30	4.27	4.18	381.7	DUNCAN	43.5	1.42	12.14	12.30		11.53	34
4.16		12.50	4.40	4.31	386.4	ESCALANTE	38.8	1.30	11.59	12.12		11.32	43
4.53 / 4.58		1.15	4.53	4.46	392.3	D DOMINGUEZ (Ms)	32.9	1.15	11.40	11.52		11.08	○ 32
5.21		1.47	5.11	5.05	399.2	D BRIDGEPORT (Bg)	26.0	12.56	11.20	11.28		10.39	55
5.40		2.10	5.22	5.18	403.9	DEER RUN	21.3	12.44	11.05	11.12		10.20	47
6.01		2.34	5.35	5.32	409.1	KAHNAH	16.1	12.29	10.49	10.52		9.58	23
6.18		2.52	5.46	5.42	412.9	N WHITEWATER (Wr)	12.3	12.18	10.38	10.37		9.42	O Y 40
6.39		3.18	6.00	5.56	418.3	UNAWEEP	6.9	12.03	10.20	10.12		9.18	○ 44
7.05		3.50	6.15 / 7.15	6.15 / 7.00	425.2	N GRAND JUNC. (Jn)		11.46 / 11.30	10.00 / 8.45	9.40		8.50	● O Y § 230
(11.45)	(0.06)	(10.55)	(6.50)	(7.07)	(184.9)		(134.9)	(6.40)	(7.87)	(11.90)	(0.05)	(12.15)	

No train shall leave Gunnison, Cimarron, Cerro Summit, Montrose or Grand Junction without special order or clearance ticket.

West-bound trains will not leave Sapinero without special order or clearance ticket.

Water Tanks at Elk Creek, 5 miles west of Kezar, and at mile 322.

FOURTH DIVISION—La Veta and Chama—FIRST AND SECOND DISTRICTS.

WESTWARD — EASTWARD

TIME-TABLE 16 — Nov. 9, 1890.

WESTWARD 441 Local Freight (Third Class) Leave Daily Exc. Sunday A.M.	431 Garland and Alamosa Freight (First Class) Leave Daily Exc. Sunday P.M.	403 Denver and Durango Passenger (First Class) Leave Daily Exc. Sunday A.M.	Miles from Denver	STATIONS AND SIDINGS	Miles from Chama	EASTWARD 404 Alamosa and Denver Passenger (First Class) Arrive Daily Exc. Sunday P.M.	432 Alamosa and Garland Freight (Third Class) Arrive Daily Exc. Sunday P.M.	442 Local Freight (Third Class) Arrive Daily Exc. Sunday P.M.	Siding capacity
			190.9	X **LA VETA** D / 8.4	151.9				○ 125
			199.3	OJO / 2.7	143.5				○ 13
			202.0	MULE SHOE / 3.8	140.8				28
			205.6	Va **VETA PASS** D / 1.7	137.2				X 33
			207.3	BLANCA / 5.2	135.5				○ 22
			212.5	Pr **PLACER** D / 7.0	130.3				●○ X 55
			219.5	TRINCHERA / 6.7	123.3				31
	1.45		226.2	Ft **GARLAND** D / 12.1	116.6	1.00			○ 37
	f 2.22		238.3	BALDY / 8.5	104.5	f 12.20			○ 39
	f 2.50		246.8	HAYES / 3.5	96.0	f 11.55			35
7.00	3.00	¶ 10.45 / 11.10	250.3	N **ALAMOSA** As / 5.3	92.5	6.00 / 5.30 ¶	11.45	6.30	●○ Y § X 211
8.00			255.6	HENRY / 9.1	87.2				○ 6
9.00 / 10.00		f 11.43	264.7	Jr **LA JARA** / 14.3	78.1	f 4.57		5.30	○ 29
		12.15 / 12.25	279.0	Na **ANTONITO** D / 10.5	63.8	**4.25 / 4.17**		**4.30 / 4.05**	○ Y 91
11.00		12.52	289.5	LAVA / 8.8	53.3	3.51		3.05	○ 26
11.50		f 1.14	298.1	BIGHORN / 6.7	44.7	3.28		2.15	29
12.25		s 1.36	304.8	Su SUBLETTE / 4.4	38.0	s 3.04		1.36	●○ 23
1.00		s 1.50	309.2	TOLTEC / 4.6	33.6	s 2.50		1.00	○ 26
		2.05 / 2.07	313.8	TOLTEC GORGE / 3.3	29.0	2.35 / 2.33			
2.20 / 2.25		s **2.20**	317.1	Bc **OSIER** D / 3.7	25.7	**2.20**		12.10	●○ X 61
2.50		f 2.34	320.8	LOS PINOS / 8.5	22.0	2.06		11.50	○ 17
3.50		s 3.00	329.3	Br **CUMBRES** D / 1.7	13.5	s 1.42		11.00	●○ Y X 30
4.05		f 3.08	331.0	COXO / 3.2	11.8	f 1.32		10.30	○ 18
4.30		f 3.20	334.2	CRESCO / 4.5	8.6	f 1.14		9.30	18
5.00		3.38	338.7	LOBATO / 4.1	4.1	12.55		8.40	○ 28
5.40		¶ 3.55 / 4.20	342.8	Ch **CHAMA** D	(151.9)	12.35 / 12.10 ¶		8.00	●○ Y § X 116
P.M. Arrive Daily Exc. Sunday (10.40)	P.M. Arrive Daily Exc. Sunday (1.15)	P.M. Arrive Daily Exc. Sunday (4.45)				Leave Daily Exc. Sunday (4.55)	A.M. Leave Daily Exc. Sunday (1.15)	A.M. Leave Daily Exc. Sunday (10.30)	

CAR CAPACITY OF SIDINGS, LOCATION OF SCALES, WATER, FUEL AND TURNING STATIONS.

No train shall leave Alamosa or Chama, without special order or clearance ticket.

No siding at Toltec Gorge.

20

FOURTH DIVISION—Chama and Durango—THIRD DISTRICT.

WESTWARD / EASTWARD

TIME-TABLE 16 — Nov. 9, 1890.

CAR CAPACITY OF SIDINGS, LOCATION OF SCALES, WATER, FUEL AND TURNING STATIONS.	Third Class (W)	451 Local Freight — Leave Daily Exc. Sunday A.M.	403 Denver and Durango Mail — Leave Daily Exc. Sunday P.M.	MILES FROM DENVER	STATIONS AND SIDINGS	MILES FROM DURANGO	404 Durango and Denver Mail — Arrive Daily Exc. Sunday P.M.	452 Local Freight — Arrive Daily Exc. Sunday P.M.	Third Class (E)
116 × § Y ○●		7.40	3.55 / 4.20	342.8	D CHAMA Ch	107.4	f 12.35 / 12.10	6.00	
					5.1				
1: ○		8.10	f 4.34	347.9	WILLOW CREEK	102.3	f 11.57	5.20	
					4.8				
38 ○		8.55	f 4.46	352.7	AZOTEA	97.5	f 11.44	4.46	
					9.5				
80 § ○		10.20	s 5.10	362.2	MONERO	88.0	s 11.21	3.25	
					3.3				
31 Y		11.08	s 5.23	365.5	D AMARGO Fc	84.7	s 11.08	2.45	
					6.5				
27		11.40	5.42	372.0	DULCE	78.2	10.50	2.00	
					4.4				
46 ○		12.00	f 5.54	376.4	□ NAVAJO Jo	73.8	f 10.38	1.35	
					9.0				
24		12.45	f 6.19	385.4	JUANITA	64.8	f 10.13	12.45	
					8.4				
41		1.30	f 6.42	393.8	CARRACAS	56.4	f 9.49	12.02	
					8.5				
40 ●●		2.10	s 7.05	402.3	D ARBOLES Ao	47.9	s 9.26	11.22	
					7.2				
19 ○		2.45	7.25	409.5	VALLEJO	40.7	9.05	10.45	
					8.2				
28 ○		3.20	7.47	417.7	LA BOCA	32.5	s 8.44	10.05	
					6.7				
32 ●○○		3.55	s 8.06	424.4	D IGNACIO Ig	25.8	s 8.25	9.30	
					11.8				
31 ○		4.50	f 8.37	436.0	FLORIDA	14.2	f 7.54	8.30	
					5.7				
		5.18	f 8.53	441.7	□ LA PLATA JUNCTION Pt	8.5	f 7.37	8.05	
					2.9				
26		5.30	9.00	444.6	□ BOCEA Bz	5.6	f 7.30	7.50	
					5.6				
302 × § ○●		6.00	9.15	450.2	D DURANGO Du		7.15	7.20	
		P.M. Arrive Daily Exc. Sunday (10.20)	P.M. Arrive Daily Exc. Sunday (4.55)		(107.4)		A.M. Leave Daily Exc. Sunday (4.55)	A.M. Leave Daily Exc. Sunday (10.40)	

No train shall leave Chama or Durango without special order or clearance ticket.

Gato Water Tank at Mile Post 389.

CONDENSED SCHEDULE OF PASSENGER TRAINS.

EASTWARD.

Nov. 9, 1890.	HOURS FROM DENVER.
DENVER	
COLORADO SP'S	5 = 2.35
COLORADO SP'S	8 = 8.00
MANITOU	
PUEBLO	5 = 4.00
FLORENCE	5 = 5.15
COAL CREEK	1 = 6.55
CANON	5 = 5.30
SALIDA	3 = 9.05
SALIDA	
LEADVILLE	7 = 11.55
DILLON	7 = 16.01
RED CLIFF	7 = 13.35
ASPEN	7 = 18.40
PONCHA JUNC.	1 = 10.24
MONARCH	3 = 14.50
MEARS JUNC.	3 = 10.01
HOT SPRINGS	3 = 11.24
GUNNISON	1 = 14.24
CRESTED BUTTE	1 = 26.00
SAPINERO	1 = 15.51
LAKE CITY.	3 = 23.41
MONTROSE	1 = 18.28
OURAY	3 = 21.25
GRAND JUNC.	3 = 21.45
SALT LAKE	1 = 83.40
OGDEN	1 = 87.10
PUEBLO	5 = 4.00
CUCHARA JUNC.	11 = 6.05
TRINIDAD	11 = 7.85
LA VETA	11 = 7.40
ALAMOSA	3 = 18.15
DEL NORTE	3 = 15.30
ANTONITO	3 = 14.45
ESPANOLA	3 = 18.30
SANTA FE	3 = 28.45
CHAMA	3 = 18.25
DURANGO	3 = 23.45
SILVERTON	3 = 28.10
IRONTON	3 = 40.30

WESTWARD.

Nov. 9, 1890.	MILES FROM DENVER.
DENVER	
COLORADO SP'S	75.1
COLORADO SP'S	80.5
MANITOU	
PUEBLO	119.6
FLORENCE	152.5
COAL CREEK	155.0
CANON	160.6
SALIDA	216.5
SALIDA	216.5
LEADVILLE	277.4
DILLON	318.3
RED CLIFF	299.5
ASPEN	407.8
PONCHA JUNC.	221.5
MONARCH	237.2
MEARS JUNC.	227.4
HOT SPRINGS	255.4
GUNNISON	290.3
CRESTED BUTTE	318.0
SAPINERO	315.7
LAKE CITY.	352.4
MONTROSE	358.2
OURAY	389.1
GRAND JUNC.	425.2
SALT LAKE	716.7
OGDEN	758.6
PUEBLO	119.6
CUCHARA JUNC.	169.3
TRINIDAD	210.6
LA VETA	190.9
ALAMOSA	250.3
DEL NORTE	281.5
ANTONITO	279.0
ESPANOLA	370.0
SANTA FE	408.4
CHAMA	342.8
DURANGO	450.2
SILVERTON	495.4
IRONTON	515.4

This time-table is based on the 24-hour system, the day beginning at midnight—24 o'clock. The hours from 1 o'clock in the morning, are numbered consecutively from 1 to 24.

A heavy line under the name of a station denotes a junction point; a double line the end of a branch.

The number at the left of the time denotes the hour, and at the right of the time denotes the train number making the quickest and most direct connection.

A double line in the "Schedule" denotes the beginning of the run of Eastward trains and the end of the run of Westward trains.

Trains of the First Division are numbered in series from 1 to 200. Second Division 201 to 300. Third Division 300, Fourth Division 401 to 500.

Through Trains, from one Division to another, and the opposing trains, carry their original number to end of run.

With the exception of Manitou Branch, local main line mixed trains and Nos. 381 and 386, the unit figure of train number indicates the Denver train with which it connects. The Denver train with which it connects thus: 488, 478 and 468 connect with 204, 364, 374 and 394 with No. 264; 204, 334, 364, 374 and 394 with 204, with 204.

*Daily except Sunday. †Monday, Wednesday and Friday. ‡Tuesday, Thursday and Saturday.

26

143

TABLE OF DISTANCES BETWEEN JUNCTION AND TERMINAL STATIONS IN MILES.

STATIONS		Colorado Springs	Manitou	Pueblo	Florence	Coal Creek	Canon	West Cliff	Salida	Leadville	Dillon	Aspen	Monarch	Hot Springs	Gunnison	Crested Butte	Montrose	Ouray	Grand Junction	Cuchara	Trinidad	Alamosa	W. W. Gap	Antonito	Espanola	Durango	Silverton
	Denver	75	81	120	153	155	161	194	217	277	313	408	237	255	290	318	353	389	425	169	211	250	311	279	370	450	495
	Denver	Colorado Springs	5	44	77	80	86	119	141	202	238	333	162	180	215	243	278	314	350	94	136	175	236	204	295	375	420
CASTLE ROCK	33	Castle Rock	Manitou	50	83	85	91	124	147	208	243	338	168	185	221	248	284	319	356	100	141	181	241	209	300	381	426
COLORADO CITY	78	45	Colorado City	Pueblo	33	35	41	74	97	158	194	288	118	136	171	198	234	270	306	50	91	131	191	159	250	331	376
PUEBLO	120	87	47	Pueblo	Florence	3	8	41	64	125	161	255	85	103	138	166	201	237	273	83	124	164	224	192	283	364	409
COAL CREEK	155	122	83	35	Coal Creek	Coal Creek	11	44	67	127	163	258	87	105	140	168	203	239	275	85	126	166	227	195	286	366	411
BUENA VISTA	242	209	170	122	92	Buena Vista	Canon	33	56	117	153	247	77	95	130	157	193	229	265	91	132	172	232	200	292	372	417
LEADVILLE	277	245	205	158	127	36	Leadville	West Cliff	86	147	183	278	107	125	160	188	223	259	295	124	165	205	265	234	325	405	450
ROBINSON	294	261	221	174	144	52	16	Robinson	Salida	61	97	191	21	39	74	102	137	173	209	147	188	228	288	256	347	428	473
RED CLIFF	300	267	227	180	150	58	28	48	Red Cliff	Leadville	36	136	82	100	135	162	198	234	270	208	249	289	349	317	408	488	534
GLENWOOD	367	334	294	247	217	125	95	111	67	Glenwood	Dillon	172	118	136	171	198	234	269	306	243	285	324	385	353	444	524	570
CARBONDALE	379	347	307	260	229	137	107	124	80	13	Carbondale	Aspen	212	230	265	293	328	364	400	338	379	419	479	446	539	619	664
A. & W. MINES	389	357	317	270	239	147	122	138	90	23	10	A. & W. Mines	Monarch	50	85	112	147	183	219	167	209	248	310	277	368	448	493
VILLA GROVE	247	215	175	128	97	56	92	108	114	181	194	204	Villa Grove	Hot Springs	91	119	154	190	226	186	227	267	328	295	386	466	512
CRESTED BUTTE	318	285	246	198	168	127	162	179	185	252	264	274	110	Crested Butte	Gunnison	28	63	99	135	220	262	301	362	330	421	501	547
DALLAS	376	343	304	256	226	185	220	237	242	310	322	332	168	113	Dallas	Crested Butte	91	127	163	248	289	329	390	358	449	529	574
SALT LAKE	717	689	645	597	567	526	561	578	583	651	663	673	509	454	386	Salt Lake	Montrose	36	72	283	325	364	425	393	484	564	609
OGDEN	754	721	681	634	603	562	598	614	620	687	700	710	546	491	423	37	Ogden	Ouray	108	319	361	400	461	429	520	600	645
BESSEMER	121	89	49	2	37	124	159	176	182	249	261	271	129	200	258	599	635	Bessemer	Grand Junction	355	397	436	497	465	556	636	681
EL MORO	206	174	134	87	122	209	245	261	267	334	347	356	214	285	343	684	720	85	El Moro	Cuchara	41	81	142	110	201	281	326
TRINIDAD	211	178	138	91	126	213	249	265	271	338	351	360	219	289	347	688	725	89	4	Trinidad	Trinidad	122	183	151	242	322	367
WALSENS	176	143	104	56	92	179	214	231	236	304	316	326	184	255	313	654	698	55	44	48	Walsen	Alamosa	61	29	120	200	245
LA VETA	191	158	119	71	107	194	229	246	251	318	331	341	199	270	328	669	705	70	59	63	15	La Veta	W. W. Gap	89	180	260	303
MONTE VISTA	268	235	195	148	183	270	306	322	328	395	408	418	273	346	404	745	788	146	135	140	92	77	Monte Vista	Antonito	91	171	216
TRES PIEDRAS	314	281	241	194	229	316	352	368	374	441	454	464	322	392	450	791	828	192	181	186	138	123	81	Tres Piedras	Espanola	262	307
SANTA FE	410	377	338	290	326	413	448	465	470	538	550	559	418	489	547	888	924	289	278	282	234	219	177	97	Santa Fe	Durango	45
CHAMA	343	310	270	223	259	346	381	397	403	470	483	493	351	422	480	821	857	222	211	215	167	152	110	98	195	Chama	Silverton
MONERO	362	330	290	243	278	365	400	417	423	490	502	512	370	441	499	840	876	241	230	234	186	171	128	118	214	19	

TABLE OF DISTANCES BETWEEN PRINCIPAL SHIPPING POINTS IN MILES.

Frontispiece of the *Official Guide for the Denver & Rio Grande Railroad* for July of 1896 was rather fancy. Users had to pay $.50 per annum for their monthly issue, and it was a large publication. Note how inexpensively the Albany Hotel fed and lodged its clients. *Colorado Historical Society*

A REALITY

On May 21, 1949 the *California Zephyr* dream became a reality. The Burlington handled it in both directions from Chicago to Denver; the Rio Grande handled it to Salt Lake City; and, the Western Pacific handled it from that point to San Francisco. The original consist was 11 cars, but the train became so popular that by 1952 the three partner railroads purchased six additional all-room (no berth or roomette) Pullmans, bringing each train's consist to 12 cars.

As 1970 approached, the Western Pacific had financial trouble. It petitioned the Interstate Commerce Commission to be allowed to drop its portion of the *California Zephyr* arrangement and route. On March 15, 1970, the permission was granted. The Burlington and Rio Grande continued to run the *Zephyr* on a tri-weekly schedule, and passengers still patronized it between Chicago and Salt Lake City.

AMTRAK

Amtrak was conceived and foisted on the tax-paying public. The Burlington accepted the Amtrak contract, but the Rio Grande refused to sign a contract that would have taken control of its profitable freight train operations and imposed rules and qualifications on its program of track maintenance and structures.

Since it was apparent that permission could not be obtained to abandon the *California Zephyr* between Denver and Salt Lake City, in lieu of signing, the Rio Grande committed itself to operate a *Rio Grande Zephyr* between these points. The schedule was tri-weekly with no train service on Wednesdays. Later, when the Burlington Northern-Union Pacific route for

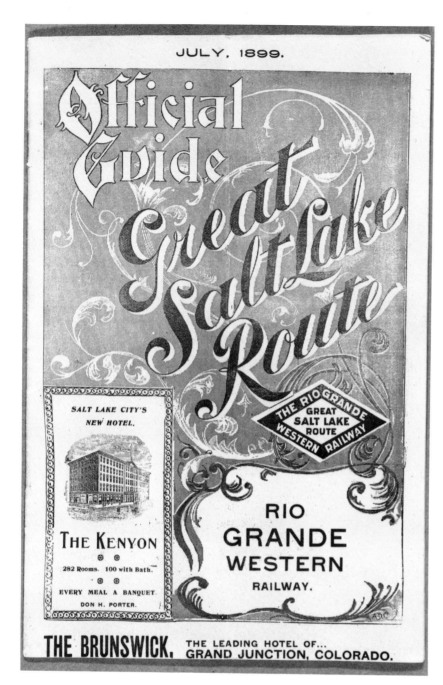

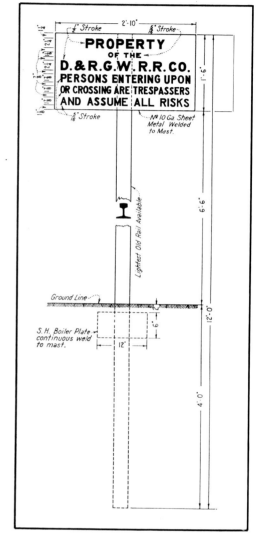

Amtrak's *Zephyr* proved unpopular, Amtrak caved in and accepted the Rio Grande's contract provisions. It would again operate over Rio Grande's tracks, through scenery that encouraged sales. About the time service began, the great earth slide in Spanish Fork Canyon at Thistle, Utah closed the tracks on April 14, 1983. The tracks were re-opened on July 4, 1983, and Amtrak resumed the schedule of its trains on the Rio Grande's segment.

RIO GRANDE ZEPHYR

During the time that the *Rio Grande Zephyr* was operated, G.B. Aydelott, Rio Grande's president, insisted that the class and quality of service given on the *Rio Grande Zephyr* rival that of the earlier *California Zephyr*'s service, even though the *Rio Grande Zephyr* had only five cars. During the life of the *Rio Grande*

Zephyr, management never received a single complaint about its food, sleeping-car condition or any other matter related to passenger service.

Leaving Denver or Salt Lake City in the mornings, passengers eagerly waited to eat in the dining car. Passengers could sit at a table covered in stiff white linen, graced by a vase of Colorado carnations and gleaming silver. Aromatic coffee, lightly touched with chicory and served in a silver pot, was served while diners read the menu.

A favorite breakfast choice was *California Zephyr* french toast with a side order of crisp, golden bacon, country sausage or ham. At lunch, the diner had a choice of several hot and cold entrees. The chicken, shrimp or crab salads elicited many compliments. At

ABOVE. Eastward bound *California Zephyr* downgrade at Rollinsville, Colorado with three diesel units (the middle B unit is an early FT model) and six passenger cars. *Colorado Historical Society*

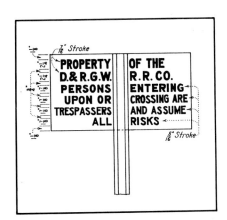

RIGHT. An earlier day meet between the westbound and eastbound *California Zephyrs* in Glenwood Canyon. The equipment is still shiny new, and the trains' consist includes some cars that were not typical *Zephyr* equipment. The diner *Silver Hostel* is in the rear portion of the westbound train. *Colorado Historical Society*

The cuisine of the *California Zephyr* was world renowned. *Colorado Historical Society*

dinner, the steaks were a gourmet's dream and were served sizzling hot. Steak knives were never stocked on the dining car because the meat was so tender that to use a steak knife would have been sacrilege. If you ever rode the *California Zephyr*, you never forgot it.

Many people have asked for the recipe of *California Zephyr* French Toast. Here it is:

CALIFORNIA ZEPHYR FRENCH TOAST

2 slices of bread, at least one day old   Butter
Eggs, beaten not whipped

Take the bread and dip each piece in the beaten egg. Lay one slice on a medium-hot griddle greased with butter. Lay the second slice on top of this. When the bottom layer is golden brown, flip the slices over and brown the top slice. The center egg will be cooked to a consistency of soft scrambled eggs.

Excursion Trains

A decade after the Civil War, railroads began soliciting and running many excursion trains. This remained a favorite business of railroads and was well-received by the public up until World War I. After that, roads and highways began improving, and automobiles became the more popular means of transportation.

By the time I went to work for the Rio Grande in 1937, no regular excursions were run. Occasionally, a group arranged for a car reserved for its use to be placed in the consist of a scheduled passenger train.

I did not ride the last excursion run out of Gunnison, Colorado to Cimarron and back prior to this section of narrow gauge track being taken up. The Rocky Mountain Railroad Club had two or three excursions over Cumbres Pass that I also missed. The Rio Grande eventually stopped all narrow gauge excursions, citing its concern over economics and safety.

During the years that I was in a supervisory position, I had only one opportunity to ride a true excursion train on the Narrow Gauge. The one bona fide excursion train that I rode was operated in May 1951 from Alamosa to Durango and back. Passenger service ended on January 31, 1951.

Heavy white linen tablecloth and napkins—new ones for each setting—heavy sterling silverware—clear crystal—a trip on the *Zephyr* was remembered for a lifetime. *Colorado Historical Society*

A smooth ride, the Rocky Mountains and Utah desert scenery and hot coffee served in a silver pot with just a touch of chicory—this was what the *California Zephyr* was all about. *Colorado Historical Society*

On board the *California Zephyr* during mealtime was a delightful experience: good service, excellent food and fine scenery to view while reaching your destination. *Colorado Historical Society*

The *California Zephyr* fed them the best food, let them view magnificent scenery, gave them a smooth ride, and then bedded them for the night. *Colorado Historical Society*

Good Morning

To Insure Prompt Service Write Each Item on Meal Check
WAITERS ARE NOT PERMITTED TO TAKE ORAL ORDERS

●

Fruits   Chilled Cantaloupe 30   Sliced Oranges 35   Kadota Figs with Cream 40
Stewed Prunes with Cream 35   Fresh Peaches with Cream 40

Fruit Juices   Apple Juice 25   Fresh Orange Juice 25   Pineapple Juice 25
Grapefruit Juice 25   Tomato Juice 25

Cereals   Oatmeal, Cream of Wheat, Puffed Rice, All Bran, Bran Flakes, Corn Flakes,
Grapenuts, Shredded Wheat with Cream 35

Club Breakfasts

Includes Choice of one Fruit, Fruit Juice or Cereal with Cream and Beverage

No. 1   Creamed Chicken on Toast, Potatoes, Toast or Muffins.............................. 1.50
No. 2   Smoked Sugar Cured Ham with Two Eggs, any style, Toast or Muffins.... 1.50
No. 3   Breakfast Bacon with Two Eggs, any style, Toast or Muffins...................... 1.50
No. 4   Wheat or Corn Cakes with Bacon 1.35
No. 5   Browned Corned Beef Hash with Poached Egg, Toast or Muffins................ 1.35
No. 6   Omelette with Strawberry Preserves, Toast or Muffins............................. 1.35
No. 7   Shredded Ham with Scrambled Eggs 1.35
No. 8   Two Eggs, any style, Toast or Muffins 1.15
No. 9   One Egg with Two Strips of Breakfast Bacon, Toast or Muffins.................... 1.15
No. 10   French Toast with Syrup or Jelly 1.00
No. 11   Fruit or Fruit Juice, Cereal with Cream, Toast or Muffins......................... .90

**Cakes, Toast
or Muffins**
   Wheat or Corn Cakes with Syrup 40
French Toast with Syrup or Jelly 60
Dry or Buttered Toast 15   Cinnamon Toast 35   Hot Muffins 15

Eggs or Entrees   Creamed Chicken on Toast 1.35   Poached Eggs on Toast 65
Two Eggs, any style 50   Smoked Ham with Two Eggs 1.25
Bacon with Two Eggs 1.25   Shredded Ham with Scrambled Eggs 85
Browned Corned Beef Hash with Poached Egg 85
Shredded Ham with Scrambled Eggs 85

Beverages   Coffee per pot 25   Hot Tea per pot 25   Cocoa per pot 25
Instant Sanka Coffee 25   Postum per pot 25   Individual Milk 15

Service Outside of Dining Car 50c extra for each Adult Person served.

Steward in Charge of this Car is...

Superintendents of Dining Car Service
P. M. Scott, Burlington, Chicago
C. A. Wall, Rio Grande, Denver
H. G. Wyman, Western Pacific, Oakland

7/50-17-18

151

BEVERAGE LIST

PRICE SHOWN INCLUDES ALL FEDERAL TAXES

Cocktails
Manhattan, Martini, Old Fashioned, Ind., 60

Wines
Imported Champagne, 13 oz. bottle, 7.25
American Sauterne, Claret, Sherry, Port, Burgundy,
  6 oz. bottle, 75—Champagne, 13 oz. bottle, 3.00
Tipo White, 8 oz., 75   Tipo Red, 8 oz., 75
Sparkling Burgundy, 13 oz., 3.00

Liquors
Bourbon Blended Ind. 1.6 oz., 55
Straight Bourbon Ind., 65   Bourbon Bonded Ind., 75
Canadian Whiskey Ind., 75
Rye Bonded 1.6 oz. Ind., 75
Scotch Imported 1.6 oz. Ind., 75-80

Highballs
Highballs with split of ginger ale, club soda or car-
  bonated water 10c extra.
Whiskey sour 10c additional charge.

Gin
Individual 1.6 oz., 50   Tom Collins, 60

Rum
Imported Ind. 1.6 oz., 75

Cordials
Benedictine Imp. 1 oz., 80   Brandy & Benedictine, 80
Creme de Menthe Ind., 65   Domestic Brandy Ind., 60
Cognac (French Brandy) 1 oz., 80

Beer
Selected Brews, bottle, 30

Ale
Domestic, Bottle, 35

Fountain Drinks
Lemonade, glass, 25   Orangeade, glass, 25
Selection of bottled soft beverages, 10
Club Soda, split, 10   Sparkling Water, split, 10
Ginger Ale, split, 10; pint, 20   Coca Cola, 15
White Rock Water, split, 15; pint, 30
Poland Water, pint, 30   Appollinaris Water, pint, 30

Cigars and Cigarettes
A selection of Domestic or Imported Cigars and
Popular Brand Cigarettes

For your protection:
Liquor and cordials are contained in individual original bottles.   Employees are
instructed to open and empty the bottles in your presence. Empty bottles to be returned
  by waiter. Sale of liquor in individual bottles to carry away is prohibited.
"Setups" will not be provided for persons furnishing their own liquor.   Sales to minors or
                persons visibly intoxicated prohibited.
The sale and service of alcoholic drinks is limited to those localities in which it is lawfully
                          permitted.

Liquor sold in the State of Colorado, 10c additional (tax)

California Zephyr

CALIFORNIA ZEPHYR

LUNCHEON

CALIFORNIA ZEPHYR

To insure Prompt Service, Please write each item on Meal Check. Waiters are not permitted to take Oral Orders.

Dinner a la Carte

RELISH . . . . .
Olives, Ripe California or Queen, 30
Fresh Pineapple Cocktail, 50
Marinated Herring, Wine Sauce, 60

SOUP . . . . .
Soup, Cup, 25; Tureen, 35

OMELETTE . . .
Plain, 75   Spanish, 90
Jelly, Marmalade, or Strawberry Preserves, 80

FISH . . . .
Filet of Lake Superior Whitefish Broiled,
Venetienne Butter 1.25

ENTREE . . . . .
Braised Swiss Steak, Brown Mushroom Sauce 1.85
Southern Fried Spring Chicken, Corn Fritter 1.50
Roast Sugar Cured Ham au Naturel,
Pineapple Ring Glace 1.60
Sugar Cured Ham and Eggs.......... 1.25
Bacon and Eggs.......... 1.25
Bread and Butter Served with Entree

SANDWICHES .
Chicken, 85; Chicken Salad, 60; Lettuce, Bacon, Tomato, 60
American Cheese, 35   Ham Sandwich, 50

VEGETABLES .
New Potatoes Rissole, 25   Au Gratin Potatoes, 30
Fresh Cauliflower, Cheese Sauce, 35   Spinach with Egg, 30

SALADS . . . . .
Chicken Salad, Mayonnaise, 1.00   Potato Salad, 35
Sliced Tomatoes, French Dressing, 60
Hearts of Lettuce, Mayonnaise, 50

BREAD . . . . .
Bread and Butter, 15   Hot Dinner Rolls, 15
Dry or Buttered Toast, 15

DESSERT . . . .
Chocolate Sundae with Wafers, 40
Fresh Peach Shortcake, Whipped Cream, 50
Ice Cream with Wafers, 35   Pear Cardinal, 40
Fleshly Baked Pie, 25   Chilled Cantaloupe, 30
Liederkranz Cheese, Toasted Wafers, 40

BEVERAGE . . .
Coffee or Tea, Pot for One, 25
Cocoa, per pot, 25   Instant Sanka Coffee, 25
Instant Postum, 25   Individual Bottle Milk, 15

The Service of all Alcoholic Beverages, including Wine and Beer, on Legal days of sale will be discontinued at 10:00 P.M.

It will be a pleasure to serve any dish not listed that you may wish if it is available.

Service Outside of Dining Car 50c extra for each Adult Person served.

Parents may share their portions with children without extra charge; or half portion served at half price to children under twelve years of age.

7/50 No. 1 - 1

Manhattan, Martini or
Old Fashioned
Cocktail, 60

American Sauterne
6 oz. Bottle, 75

Sparkling Burgundy
Half Bottle 13 oz., 3.00

Cognac
(French Brandy), 80

Brandy and
Benedictine, 80

Creme de Menthe, 65

Select Dinners

Following Items Will Be Served with Meals Listed Below at Additional Prices Shown.

Minestrone Soup, 20   Hot or Jellied Consomme, 20
Fresh Pineapple Cocktail, 35   Marinated Herring, Wine Sauce, 45

(Price Opposite each Entree Includes
Vegetable, Potatoes, Dessert, and Beverage)

Filet of Lake Superior Whitefish Broiled, Venetienne Butter........ 2.00
Braised Swiss Steak, Brown Mushroom Sauce........ 2.50
Southern Fried Spring Chicken, Corn Fritter........ 2.15
Roast Sugar Cured Ham au Naturel, Pineapple Ring Glace........ 2.25
Omelette with Chicken Liver au Madere........ 1.65

New Potatoes Rissole   Au Gratin Potatoes
Fresh Cauliflower, Cheese Sauce   Spinach with Egg

Bon Ton Salad, French Dressing
(served with these meals 25c additional)

Fresh Peach Shortcake, Whipped Cream   Chocolate Sundae with Wafers
Pear Cardinal   Blueberry Pie   Chilled Cantaloupe
Liederkranz Cheese, Toasted Wafers
Hot Rolls

Coffee   Tea   Milk   Cocoa   Iced Tea   Postum   Sanka Coffee

SPECIAL COLD PLATE $1.75

Assorted Cold Cuts with India Relish
Sliced Tomatoes, French Dressing
Potato Salad
Choice of Dessert
Hot Rolls
Coffee   Tea   Milk

FOR THE LITTLE ONES

Baby Soup .... .15   Puree of Prunes .... .15
Puree of Peas. .... .15   Apple Sauce .... .15

Steward in Charge of this Car is

Superintendents of Dining Car Service
P. M. Scott, Burlington, Chicago
C. A. Wall, Rio Grande, Denver
H. G. Wyman, Western Pacific, Oakland

Vern Hallenbeck, a banker, lumber dealer, moving spirit of Colorado Springs, and the prototype of the avid railfan, chartered a train for himself and some friends to run as soon as the snow on Cumbres melted. His party was to consist of about 75 friends who he wanted to introduce to the beauty and nostalgia of the last remaining narrow gauge main line. All costs were paid by Hallenbeck and guaranteed, so Rio Grande management agreed to run the train roundtrip from Alamosa to Durango.

Hallenbeck was almost obsessed with the Narrow Gauge. He had many friends among train and engine crew members, and he broke many rules, including the one that states no outsiders could ride the engine. You never knew when you would see an engine go by with him at the throttle. He was a competent engine handler, and to sit at the throttle of a narrow gauge engine was his idea of heaven.

Hallenbeck's train consisted of one parlor car-dinette that was not provided with meal service, two coaches and a baggage car. The baggage car had a supply of ice to keep the liquid refreshments cold. Bring your own booze was the rule of the day, and, there were few, if any, who did not follow the rule.

On this trip, Hallenbeck carried a legitimate permit to ride the engine, and he took full advantage of it. On neither day was there much freight train activity; the excursion practically had the railroad to itself. There were numerous stops at scenic or historic locations, and runbys for camera bugs. A slightly longer stop was made at Chama to pick up box lunches; this was also done on the return trip.

After the excitement of Cumbres Pass and the effects of the box lunches, the scenery west of Chama did little for the excursionists. Naps and quiet tête-à-têtes replaced the earlier excitement. Hallenbeck was tired of playing engineer, and, for the rest of the trip, he rode in the lounge car.

Leaving Gato (Pagosa Junction), Hallenbeck told me that he wanted to give a party at Durango. He informed me that he wanted dinner and drinks at the Strater Hotel in Durango for everyone, including the train and engine crew and a few special friends he had made among D&RGW personnel around Durango. I told him that this added up to nearly 100 people, and he replied, ''So what? Line it up.''

The train was stopped at Ignacio to permit me to do so by phone, and, upon arrival at Durango, Betty Evans, Hallenbeck's personal secretary, and I went to the Strater to check on arrangements. Tables were set, prime rib was in the oven and the extra help was on hand in the restaurant and bar, the Diamond Belle.

It would be a waste of words to go into detail about that evening's occasion. It was a bash. The Strater outdid itself with the food, its service and the generosity of its drinks. At the end, Hallenbeck handed his

A railfan special with Engine #487 westbound; Cresco is just in the trees to the left center of photo. State Highway #17 is on the slope above the rail line and was not even paved until about 1966. On the far skyline in the basin between the two volcanic formations is Turquoise Lake that can't be seen from the railroad. *Dr. Richard Severance*

purse to me and instructed his secretary to go with me and settle the bill. It was a fat purse, containing a few thousand dollar and a lot more hundred dollar bills. After the account was settled, the purse was a much leaner one.

The return trip the next day was more leisurely. Most people on the train did not awaken until we reached Chama. Hallenbeck did not ride on the engine on the return trip. Upon arrival at Alamosa, a trainload of tired and happy excursionists disembarked. Hallen-

beck was jubilant and later presented me with a custom-made, big game rifle that I still use.

When the Rio Grande was trying to abandon the Silverton Branch, Hallenbeck was our most vociferous and adamant opponent. I will always believe he was instrumental in stopping the abandonment. Many railfans of the past, present and future and the city of Durango, owe Vern Hallenbeck, the first and most dedicated narrow gauge fan, a rousing vote of thanks.

Oil tank cars leave westbound from Alamosa with a doubleheader in June of 1959. The Extra train is pulled by locomotives #486-487. *M.D. McCarter collection*

Both #486 and #487 load up on coal at Antonito, Colorado in 1959 prior to assaulting the grades over Cumbres Pass. The Pass will command the attention of the train crew and the wherewithall from the locomotives' boiler and drivers to climb the steep mountains to the west. *M.D. McCarter collection*

Double headed freight with tank cars pounds the iron near Alamosa. *M.D. McCarter collection*

Freight Movement between Alamosa and Antonito

Before trucks began to take much of our westbound freight business, it was standard practice to make up and start our freight trains out of Alamosa soon after the daily transfer of business from standard gauge cars to narrow gauge cars was finished. This meant most departures were late in the evening when we had enough business to justify at least one freight train per day.

As trucks increasingly took business away from railroads, we had less and less westbound freight to be transferred. Consequently, we began to run fewer trains and often spent the night hours scrounging for cars to be put together in a train. Freight trains were now likely to depart Alamosa in the early morning. In many ways, this improved operations for us. Railfan photographers loved this because it permitted them to shoot rolls of photographs from the time the train was made up until it departed. Then, they could drive down Highway 285, which paralleled the railroad, and shoot several more rolls of pictures while the train was balling-the-jack to Antonito, 28 miles from Alamosa.

The fireman wasted coal so that these railfans could capture the smoke on film. The fun ended for them when the train left Antonito for the ascent to Cumbres. There were only rough, narrow, dirt roads west of Antonito, and most were not in close proximity to the railroad. This was acceptable to them because railfans thought that a daylight train from Alamosa to Antonito was heaven. Soon after the Rio Grande ceased operations between Alamosa and Durango, Eastman Kodak stock fell.

When I look at some of these pictures, I feel a great sense of nostalgia. I think of the many times I was on the highway watching the smoke roll and listening to the whistles blowing for crossings or stations. I especially remember the many times as trainmaster I rode the engine or the caboose. Unlike the railfans, I was privileged to experience the ride all the way to Chama, and on the following day, I could continue on to Durango.

The memory of the two K-36s on the headend of a string of freight cars rolling down absolutely straight track is a treasured one.

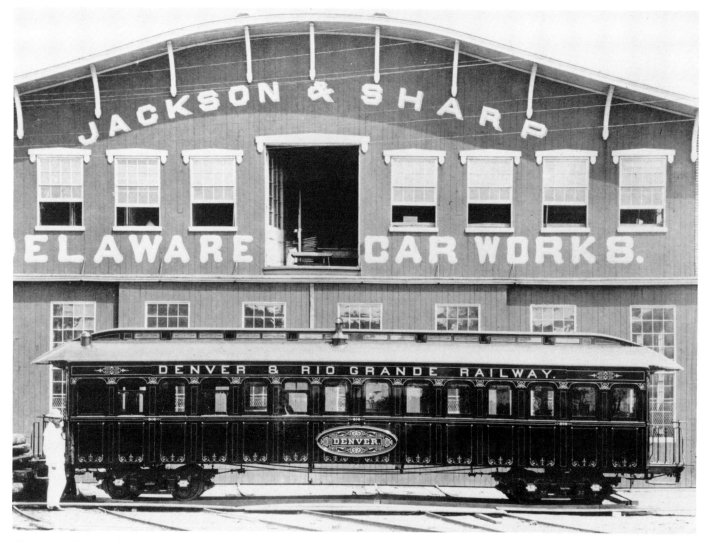

This manufacturer's photograph of the D&RG car *Denver* reveals the care this car received in the building process and the beauty it attained at completion. They don't make them like this anymore. Jackson & Sharp was the builder. *Colorado Historical Society*

Chapter 6

Equipment

Equipment on the D&RG

Jackson & Sharp, carbuilders of Wilmington, Delaware, built four cars for William Jackson Palmer's not yet completed railroad between Denver and Colorado Springs during 1870-1871. When completed and shipped to Denver, they comprised the equipment of the first excursion on October 26, 1871 from Denver to Colorado Springs.

There were two coaches, the Denver and El Paso; a smoker, No. 3; and a baggage-mail car, No.4. There is not much history on car Nos. 3 and 4. The Denver

later was converted to business car M; the El Paso was converted to business car K. Both cars were narrow gauge.

Business car K may have been assigned to William H. Jackson when he was on assignment for the D&RG. This car appears in pictures that Jackson shot for Otto Mears on Lizard Head Pass in 1895.

During the early years of the D&RG, Jackson & Sharp built other cars for Palmer. The quality of materials and craftsmanship of their products were superb.

The Salida barrel transfer was named in reference to the barrel shape of the car turning mechanism. *Denver Public Library, Western History Section*

Salida Barrel Transfer

The barrel transfer in Salida, Colorado was used to transfer mine products from open top narrow gauge cars to standard gauge cars. A lot of coal from the Gunnison area and limestone (dolomite) from Monarch Quarry, destined to the Colorado Fuel and Iron Corporation's steel mills at Minnequa, Colorado was transferred from narrow gauge to standard gauge cars at Salida.

On February 4, 1947 two days before my 32nd

birthday, I fell from a tree and broke 13 bones. My wrecked torso was rushed to the Salida D&RGW's Company Hospital. I spent my birthday under ether while R.A. Hoover M.D., orthopedist, put the pieces back together. I was in traction for almost 90 days after being patched back together, and I had to lay on a canvas, drumtight traction bed. From my bed in the hospital, I watched the barrel transfer work.

The barrel transfer shut down when the Crested

The boilerhead of locomotive #492 was a maze of gauges, valves and pipes—but only to the untrained eye. *M.D. McCarter collection*

Butte CF&I's mine closed, and it put a lot of good men out of work. During periods of 24-hour operations, approximately 300 men were employed at the barrel transfer and did other types of transfer work. Narrow gauge to standard gauge transfer, or vice versa, was an expensive operation.

Steam Locomotives

I rode many narrow gauge steam engines, and, at times, I relieved the fireman for short periods of time. Enginemen objected because it seemed as though I could never keep the needle of the steam gauge against the peg. And, they would never let me near a shovel when the engine was dragging up the 4 percent grade from Chama to Cumbres.

Neither were they very enthusiastic about me volunteering to throw in a few scoops of coal when we were drifting downgrade toward the Los Pinos water tank. A few suggested that the train would get to Alamosa and

tie up faster if I would stay in the crummy and ride the cushions, as any self-respecting official should, and quit playing railroad. I could not argue with them because I never did learn how to keep the engine hot.

There are not many instruments or gauges on the boilerhead of a steam locomotive, but each of them is very important, and their proper use and observation are as critical to the engine's performance as the use of sophisticated instruments on a large airplane.

The monitor requiring the closest attention is the water glass. Depending upon the grade, the water level in the glass must be kept at the correct level, and, above all, it must never be allowed to get so low that no water shows, at least not when there is a fire in the firebox. The water must never get so low that when the gauge cock is opened, vapor is produced.

SLEEPING ON THE JOB

I was present once when this happened and was privileged to watch two frightened, but courageous, old-time enginemen take the necessary actions to keep the crown sheets from burning or the boiler from blowing up. The crisis was over before I knew the real danger of the situation, but when I did, I got scared, too.

It happened during the Cumbres snow blockade of 1952 when the crews were pushed to exhaustion. We tied up at Los Pinos after taking water on the engines and rotary plow. A trainman who was not as exhausted as the rest of us volunteered to act as engine watchman, claiming that he had filled in as a temporary watchman at the Durango roundhouse in the past. The enginemen tested his knowledge and agreed he knew what to do. Everyone hit the blankets.

The outfit cars were spotted on the west end of the siding with the engines on the main track opposite them. The next thing I knew, I was awakened by a loud yell from the deck of one of the engines. One of the enginemen was awakened by a bladder too full of coffee, and, while awake, he went to check his engine to see if everything was alright.

It was not. The watchman fell asleep, and, when the engineman checked the glass, it was empty. When he opened the gauge cock, it emitted a blue vapor. That was when he yelled for a brother engineman to help. That yell awakened the rest of us, so we foolishly watched. Smarter or more knowledgeable men would have taken to the woods.

QUICK ACTION

I watched as one engineman in his clothes and another in his long johns worked the shaker bar for all it was worth, dumping the fire from the firebox. I was not experienced enough to know what else they did to quickly extinguish the fire, but whatever they did, it was successful.

By this time, we realized the danger of the situation. When it was resolved, I expected those two old-timers to tear the watchman apart. They did not, but one of them said quietly, but emphatically, "Young fellow, you almost got a lot of men blown to pieces. What happened?"

The watchman had properly checked the rotary and one engine and returned to the other. He stoked the fire on the second engine and then sat down. He fell asleep before starting the injector to put water in the boiler.

Valuable working time was lost firing up the dead engine after it had cooled enough to put water back in the boiler safely. The crew members were a bit cool toward the watchman for a while, but neither they nor the two enginemen chastised him for placing everyone in jeopardy. Fortunately, no one was hurt, and there was still a lot of snow to be moved and a railroad to be opened, so why waste the time chastising him.

Me? I followed the lead of the crew members in respect to the culprit, but the joy of riding the engines and playing fireman was gone when it was brought home to me that locomotives were not playthings.

Snow Fighting Equipment

Making a passageway through deep snow was a problem on railroads from the moment the first rails were laid across the mountains. This was not

Near Hermosa, Engine #463 and her train ply the Durango-Silverton branch in March of 1950. *Denver Public Library, Western History Section*

exclusive to the D&RGW's Narrow Gauge. The need existed on the mountain lines of the Rio Grande's standard gauge, the Colorado Midland and the Colorado Southern and all other mountain railroads. Wind-driven snow on the plains caused trouble, too.

In the earlier days, men wielding shovels were used to remove snow. When the railroads matured, various types of wedge plows attached to the front of locomotives or mounted on heavily ballasted cars were used. Rotary fan-type plows were used during severe storms. At a much later date, technically sophisticated snow melters were developed, but these were not successful except in the railroad yards.

Whatever method was employed, men of iron were needed. It took guts, as well as stamina, to open the throttle of an engine equipped with a wedge and ram it into snow that was often deeper than the engine was high. This was especially true if there were two to four engines coupled together behind yours, all with the same wide-open throttle.

Not as much daredevil nerve was required for the pilot (engineer on the wheel) of a rotary. But to sit in the pilothouse of a rotary as the wheel chewed up snow and spit it out, did require fortitude, finesse, a cast-iron stomach (to ingest the many cups of coffee needed to stay alert) and an absolute freedom from claustrophobia. More importantly, it required a "feel" for what the fan was doing and whether the rotary was still riding on the rail or moving forward on an iced-over flange and heading for the tules.

NARROW GAUGE TR

An example of the C&S snow-fighting equipment. *Denver Public Library, Western History Section*

162

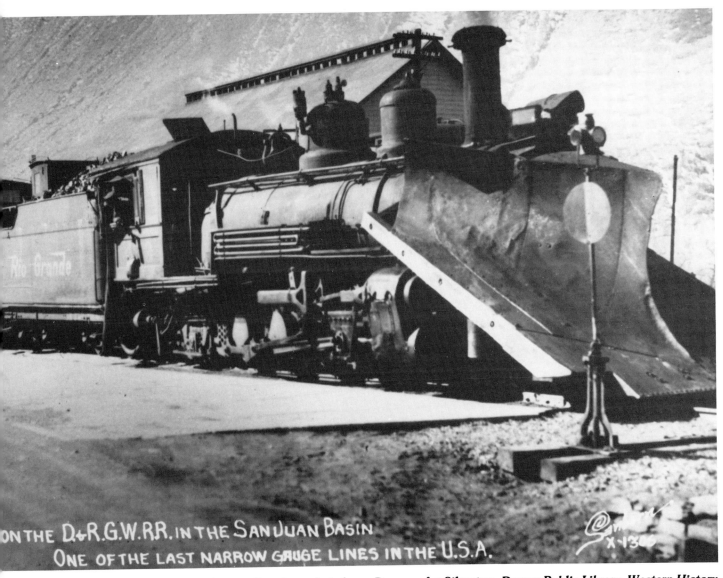

On the D.&R.G.W.RR. in the San Juan Basin
One of the last narrow gauge lines in the U.S.A.

Engine #463 with wedge snowplow in place is ready to leave Durango for Silverton. *Denver Public Library, Western History Section*

An example of Colorado Midland snow-fighting equipment, the rotary snowplow. *Denver Public Library, Western History Section*

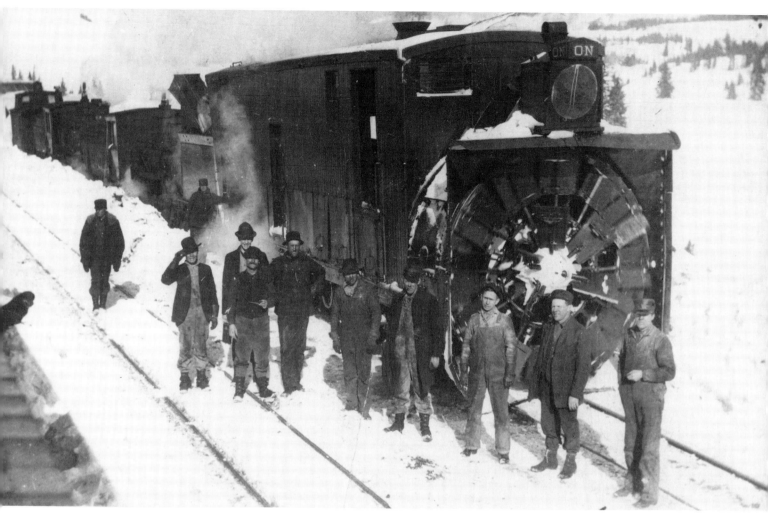

The "roadrie", as someone wrote it on the front of this picture, was a handy piece of machinery for a railroad to own. *M.D. McCarter collection*

Not every engineer had these capabilities. On the Narrow Gauge, the number of these men could be counted on 10 fingers. Those who did qualify proudly bore the title "Snow King." When a rotary train was to run, a Snow King was called regardless of his standing on the ready board or his senority. Any run-around penalties were gladly paid to get a competent Snow King in the pilothouse. If it was a prolonged tour, a second Snow King was called to deadhead and relieve the first as required.

During my assignment as trainmaster and assistant superintendent on the Alamosa Division (later Colorado), I rode on the rotaries OM and OY for hundreds of hours. The Rio Grande also had rotaries ON and OO, but I never had an opportunity to work with these. Many times, I kept the Snow King company to help keep him awake. When we had an extremely hard time moving snow, we opened a cab window, made a mark in the snow wall with a brake club, and then watched to see if we were making any progress.

Oil Tanks on Cumbres Pass

It was a rare occasion to see a short, westbound freight train on Cumbres Pass. By 1959, the Rio Grande could not afford to run such uneconomical trains. The rule was that if you could not find enough tonnage for a doubleheader, you waited until you did. Shippers did not like this, and they seldom believed that the Rio Grande was conscientiously trying to run a profitable railroad in an effort to continue operations. Later, when abandonment was imminent, reference was frequently made to delayed business. The truth is that there was a real desire on the part of the Rio Grande to save this last vestige of its founder's accomplishments.

There were never more than two producing oil fields on the Narrow Gauge. The first was in the Farmington, New Mexico, district on the Farmington Branch. A pool of oil was drilled here in the mid-1930s, and, until a refinery was built at Farmington, the district's

Durango was always one of the most well-known locations on the Narrow Gauge. It was the goal of the San Juan extension; the center of the railroad to the east, the Farmington Branch, the Silverton Branch and Otto Mears' Rio Grande Southern. Engine #493 on a very cold, snowy morning is ready to make a run to Farmington with a load of pipe for the gas fields and a tank car of gasoline.

production moved by rail to a refinery in the Denver area. The rail movement did not last long because the rate was necessarily expensive and there was the inconvenience of transferring from narrow gauge to standard gauge at Alamosa.

GRAMPS OIL

In 1935, I was working for the William E. Hughes Estate (later, the Annie Clifton Hughes Estate) on the Navajo River in Colorado about 50 miles from Chama when the first oil was struck. I originally worked as a rodman along with the geologist who surveyed the field, and later, I worked as a tool-dresser on one of the rigs. The geologist estimated the discovery would produce 8 million barrels of oil before the pool went dry. His figure was remarkably close, and the Rio Grande hauled all of it from Chama to Alamosa.

I do not know what a barrel of oil was worth then, but it was evidently enough for the Hughes Estate to build a pipeline from the field to Chama. This oil production branch was named "Gramps Oil" in honor of William E. Hughes who created the estate. In addition to the pipeline, facilities for loading the oil into tank

165

Extra #483 West is at Cumbres with a string of empty oil tanks in 1959. A crew member checks the cars. *M.D. McCarter collection*

cars from the pipeline were built on a pair of tracks at the east end of the Chama yard.

Eleven loaded tank cars made tonnage for two 480 or 490 Class engines from Chama to Cumbres. Two turns were ordinarily run, which put 22 cars of oil at Cumbres. Then, a tonnage train was run with other business, and it picked up the 22 cars of oil at Cumbres.

Gramps Oil leased UTLX tank cars, which were taken off standard gauge trucks and put on narrow gauge ones. Considering the narrow wheelbase, there should have been derailments. On some of the Cumbres' curves, crew members would sit in the cupola and watch the tanks swing and sway, wondering how they stayed on the rails.

I was away from the railroad working for the Bureau of Reclamation until late in July 1937. Gramps Oil

began to ship oil, although the leased UTLX cars were not yet painted with the big "GRAMPS" signs that were finally seen. The last oil was shipped in 1963 after a total of 481 trainloads had been shipped.

Inspection Cars

During my tenure on the Rio Grande, officers had three ways in which to make an inspection tour. They could walk; they could ride a bouncing, open-section motor car; or, they could ride in a comfortable business car or the rear platform of a passenger train. Employees on line preferred the officer to ride the business car or the platform on the rear passenger car because the train was moving so fast, the officer could not detect any problems.

M-1 motor car at Pueblo, Colorado in 1939. "I remember," wrote a D&RGW employee, "how all of us on line dreaded it when word was out this thing was on a tour of inspection." The railroad officials have their luggage strapped to the top and are all ready to go.

One of our inspection cars on the standard gauge was a Model T Ford equipped with a set of oversized, steel motor car wheels that was unfit for use on the highway. The same was true of the narrow gauge MW-02. Neither of these cars should be confused with standard gauge Inspection Car Motor No. 1, which was converted from one of Henry Ford's first V-8 sedans. It was supplied with a hydraulic jack mechanism that made it easy to move it on or off the rail, and it could operate on both highway and rail. First called a "High-Railer," it, along with similar models appearing on other railroads, soon was named the "Hy-Rail Car."

This car was almost the answer, but only four men could ride in it, and any luggage was carried on a roof rack. This made the car top-heavy and unsafe on curves at track speed. Also, the total weight, counting passengers, luggage and jack mechanisms, was too much to allow maintaining speed along the highway.

In the 1920s, one of Otto Mears' railroads at Silverton converted an open-top Model T Ford in order to operate on the Silverton Northern. This one was more successful than ours, but Mears did not run it as far as ours on any given day.

UNNECESSARY DELAY

What delayed the development of the successful Hy-Rail cars was that automobile manufacturers did not adhere to the Roman chariot gauge between wheels of 4 feet, 8$\frac{1}{2}$ inches as railroads did. Some companies used a gauge of 4 feet, 7$\frac{1}{2}$ inches for standard; others used gauges from standard to as much as one inch wider. These variations rendered conversion to rail operations very difficult.

Pontiac Manufacturers turned out a large sedan specifically for conversion to 4 feet, 8$\frac{1}{2}$ inch gauge. We liked it, but it was very heavy to lift on and off the rail. Also, it had a tendency to derail on tight curves on our branch lines. After a serious derailment in Utah, it was retired.

Dodge Manufacturers then offered a van specifically built for conversion. It worked well, and several were ordered and fitted with jack mechanisms at Dodge's plant near Kansas City, Missouri. G.B. (Gus) Aydelott, E.H. Warning and I were on an inspection trip on the Rock Island when we were told a Dodge van was to be delivered. The supervisor of roadway equipment was sent to take delivery. He met us at Fairbury, Nebraska. It was early in the day when he returned with the van, so we went by highway to Goodland, Kansas for the night.

It was snowing lightly when we departed Goodland, and the storm increased as we moved west. At Vona, 25 miles west of the Kansas-Colorado line, the road was closed due to drifting snow. Our party, along with about 75 other travelers, took refuge in a restaurant-filling station. We were there about 10 hours when we were told that a highway snowplow was en route from Burlington, Colorado for us to follow into Limon, Colorado. At the time that we were informed, there was no travel between Limon and Denver.

CIVILIZATION

The warning of the road being closed west of Vona proved true, but we were happy to be closer to civilization. The restaurant and local people of Vona kept us well-fed and warm, even though they must have severely strained their own stores for food to feed such a mob.

Arriving at Limon, Colorado, I went down to the joint Union Pacific-Rock Island station and used the telegraph to contact the Rock Island's chief dispatcher at Fairbury, Nebraska. He told me they had a snowplow train about an hour from Limon and ordered the operator to stop the snowplow and allow us to ride in the caboose from Limon to Denver. The Rock Island utilized our facilities at North Yard, Denver, so we were able to ride in an over-heated crummy on the last leg of our journey.

As pleased as we were with the Dodge, all the way from Vona, we were extremely cold and nearly frozen although the heater appeared to be operating at maxi-

Myron Henry, left, and "Punk" Blackstone at Ceder Hill, New Mexico in early 1960s when the #3000 diesel broke down. *Doug Harley collection*

mum capacity. Later, after the rig was picked up at Limon and driven to Denver for inspection, the pre-stamped blank between the heating unit and the cab had not been removed at the factory. Even though the heater was working, the heat could not flow into the cab.

That one failure did not sour us on Dodge vans' performance, and soon the Rio Grande and most other railroads had more Hy-Railers than motorcars operating. Automobile manufacturers closely adhered to standard gauge, and makers of the hydraulic jack mechanism continued to make improvements on it.

Experimental, Multi-Gauge Engines

About 1959, the U.S. Army asked the Rio Grande to test two experimental, multi-gauge, diesel-powered engines under actual operating conditions. The engines could be used on three-foot, meter or standard gauge. We were asked to do the three-foot testing.

The Rio Grande agreed, and U.S. Army experimental Engines Nos. 3000 and 4000 soon arrived and were put into service. On the run to Durango from Alamosa, they tended to rock badly, so it was decided to make all the tests on the Farmington Branch.

When we changed gauge by sliding the wheels on the axles to the desired gauge and locked them in place, the wheels were not moved equally from both sides of the engine. Thus, on one side, the wheels were off the center of balance. On the inside of curves, when the off-center side was inside the curve, the engine leaned at a disconcerting angle and caused frequent derailments. The same tendency caused the lead wheels to always fail to enter the switches properly.

These problems were more noticeable and pronounced on Engine No. 4000 than on Engine No. 3000. Engine No. 4000 was soon returned to the U.S. Army. Business was light on the Farmington Branch, and the Rio Grande patriotically suffered and completed the desired testing using Engine No. 3000. The forces at Durango survived through all the testing.

OTHER PROBLEMS

Besides derailments, there frequently were mechanical failures. After a few trial runs and rerailings, the crews soon learned the maximum speed various curves could be negotiated while keeping the engine on the rail. Maximum curvature on the Farmington Branch was 7 degrees. After a period of time, it was possible to make several trips without a derailment. During this same period, crews learned that the engine would properly track going through switches if the move was made from a stopped position or at a very slow speed.

Coming to the Rio Grande at about the same time as

the two test engines was Lieutenant Colonel Hoteen Huff from Fort Eustis, Virginia (the U.S. Army railroad training and development center). He was on a one year assignment to learn about railroad organization and operations. At the time, I was assigned as the assistant superintendent of the Colorado division.

For one year, he was my shadow regardless of time, location or weather conditions. His presence, initially accepted with reluctance, developed into one of my most pleasurable experiences. I often think I learned as much from Huff as he learned from me.

I regretted his return to Fort Eustis, but he was soon replaced by Captain Tom McDermott, who was also going to learn the ins and outs of railroading. McDermott was a nice fellow, but he usually got lost when traveling around Denver. Frequently, we had to send someone to bring him back to the railroad. After about three months, he transferred to another division of the U.S. Army.

Converting Cars from Standard to Narrow Gauge

There are many more differences between standard and narrow gauge track than just distance between rails. This was never more readily apparent than in the Rio Grande terminal at Alamosa where narrow gauge started toward the San Juan area. Actually, it was dual gauge on the 30-mile segment between Alamosa and Antonito, Colorado.

Almost all tracks in the Alamosa Yard were dual gauge, but there were enough exceptions at a few locations to result occasionally in an engine or cars running out of railroad. This was especially true during the fall when business increased. When this happened, we had to borrow men from one of the standard gauge divisions. Since nearly all our switch engines were standard gauge, most of the derailments occurred when someone tried to run a standard gauge engine down a narrow gauge track. This usually occurred when a hostler or inexperienced trainman tried to move a standard gauge engine out of the way or took a wrong route going against a madeup train.

Another problem area was at our stockyards at Alamosa. They were built on our west wye (there was an east wye across the Rio Grande River using the Hooper Branch as one leg). In order to spot cars to load or unload stock to or from the Narrow Gauge, it was necessary to first shove the cars up the Creede Branch then cut off the engine. Once the engine was removed, it was taken down the tracks leading into Antonito, backed against the narrow gauge cars, and then pulled them through to spot at the proper stock chute. Similar operating situations occurred at Salida and Montrose, except their stockyards were not built on a wye.

Rail and rail fittings on the Narrow Gauge were lighter in weight, which made it possible to still use men to lay track or make track repairs. This and the gauge meant that we never had any mechanized track equipment. Ties were shorter, and girth measurement was less than standard gauge. During the last years, it became almost impossible to buy narrow gauge ties, so standard gauge ones were used.

By 1954, the only narrow gauge operating was west of Alamosa, so the pace in the yards slowed. After the Farmington pipe movement was over, except in stock season, service seldom required more than one train a day. Consequently, if there was a washout, blockade or derailment, it was not as urgent to reopen the line to prevent traffic delays.

On the standard gauge, there was a constant drive for improved techniques, increased speed and improvement of equipment—an image of building for the future. But on the Narrow Gauge, old techniques were adequate, existing equipment was kept operable, and no new equipment was introduced. The Narrow Gauge was doomed.

REFURBISHING

Excluding the period during the Farmington pipe movement when there was much work done and money spent converting some standard gauge box cars to open-ended narrow gauge gondolas, the conversion of many narrow-gauge, flat bottom coal cars to open-ends and the strengthening of existing narrow gauge flatcars, very little money, was spent on equipment, with one exception.

In November 1935 trustees took over the property, and the Rio Grande did not need to comply with bond interest and maturity problems until reorganization was completed. The two trustees planned and executed heavy, physical rehabilitation. Plant, freight and passenger equipment shared in the program. Maybe because the equipment was smaller or because it was considered an appropriate warming up exercise, one of the first projects was to upgrade and improve 14 narrow gauge locomotives and 38 passenger cars.

The cars were refurbished and put in service during the summer of 1937. From worn-out, frowzy, Toonerville cars, they were transformed into glamour girls. Instead of coal-burning, cast iron heaters, there was now steam heat. Instead of kerosene lamps, there were electric lights. The open-ended platforms now had vestibuled ends.

The coaches were now equipped with upholstered, reclining seats with footrests—just like the big boys. Three cars, the Alamosa, Chama and Durango, were equipped with individual, movable, upholstered chairs and a dining section that could seat four people at a time. Compact, well-designed galleys built of stainless steel were used to prepare food and drink. The attendant-chef jobs on these cars attracted some of our

This was the scene at the Alamosa Station in September 1949 as standard gauge and narrow gauge sat side by side; two worlds apart, yet the same.
M.D. McCarter collection

A construction train along with a number of workers is on the old LaVeta Pass line at the muleshoe at the foot of the pass on the east side. *Colorado Historical Society*

more venerable and gracious Dining Car Department employees.

It hardly seems possible, but I think they served better meals than their compatriots on the *California Zephyr*. At least, I'll take the oath that steaks on the Narrow Gauge were better.

These three cars were assigned and used on the *San Juan* between Alamosa and Durango. Two similar parlor cars, the Salida and the Gunnison, were assigned to the *Shavano*, running between Salida and Gunnison.

Trying to compete with the standard gauge, each of the five cars was equipped with an illuminated sign that was integrated with the rear platform railing structure and design. These signs were circular in shape and similar to a drumhead. The face was a skillfully executed mountain scene that illuminated when its switch was turned on. The words "Denver and Rio Grande Western" were around the border except at the bottom where the *San Juan* or *Shavano* train name appeared.

The *Shavano* made its last run over Marshall Pass on November 24, 1940. The beautifully refurbished equipment was used on the Alamosa-Durango-Silverton territory as needed. Occasionally, it was necessary to use one of the *Shavano*'s parlor cars on the rear of the *San Juan*. On such occasion, the *Shavano* sign appeared on the rear car. The *San Juan*'s last run was on January 31, 1951, and thereafter, neither sign was lit ever again.

Construction Trains

It is very difficult to believe that the first transcontinental railroad, built by the Central Pacific and the Union Pacific from Omaha, Nebraska to Sacramento, California, conquered all obstacles including the Sierra Mountains using mostly man-powered equipment. As monumental as this was, five years later, the Rio Grande opened the Rocky Mountain Empire and overcame obstacles just as great using similar equipment.

The first passenger train was run on the Denver & Rio Grande Railway from Denver to Colorado Springs on October 26, 1871. Part of its consist included coaches and a baggage and mail car all built continental style with two-wheel trucks. This wheel configuration was never satisfactory, and the proud pieces of passenger train equipment were soon relegated to construction train service as officer cars. There is no information as to the length of time they were used as office cars.

Building progress was slow for many reasons. The rails reached La Veta, Colorado in July 1876, but did 1877. Wagon Creek (Russell) was reached July 1, 1877 and 30 days later rail's end was at Garland City (a construction temporary town) about seven miles east of the community and military post of Fort Garland. There, for lack of monies and difficulties at the Royal Gorge west of Pueblo, construction was halted, and Alamosa was not reached until July 1878. Again, delays occurred when building toward Santa Fe and Durango. Tracklaying did not resume until February 1880.

ENGINE NO. 65

In the interim, the company worked at upgrading the hastily and often inadequately built track over La Veta Pass, which was still in progress into the early 1880s. One of the engines used during this work was Engine No. 65. It was a Baldwin product built in March 1880 that weighed, fully loaded with fuel and water, only 24 tons. The proud, new engine was put to work in other than a glamourous occupation. If business was booming, such a new engine would not have been assigned to construction work.

At Mule Shoe Curve where the ascending grade over Old La Veta Pass begins, a stonework bridge was built that required betterment. Just west of this bridge, a steep-sloped hillside of a loosely compacted deposit of disintegrated rock required a lot of work over and above what was originally done. Engine No. 65 was assigned to the construction crews involved in these two chores.

ENGINE NO. 101

A unique engine that was used for handling construction trains on Old La Veta Pass was a Fairlee two-ended locomotive built in England. In an effort to influence financial centers to loan him money, William Jackson Palmer authorized his agent, W.A. Bell, to purchase an engine from Robert F. Fairlee. It was built in the Vulcan Foundry at Lincolnshire, England. It arrived in Denver on June 20, 1873 and was given D&RG Engine No. 101 and named the *Mountaineer*.

Engine No. 101 had many faults. Because of its troublesome record on the D&RG, it was the only one ever brought to the United States. The D&RG modified it in many ways and built an auxiliary water-fuel car using a flatcar on which a large pickle vat was used to hold water and a heavy box to hold extra fuel. The

RIGHT. Perhaps the same train shown on the previous page, the flat cars are better seen in this picture. The grade line on opposite side of the valley is the wagon road from Walsenberg-La Veta into the San Luis Valley. The cut where the train is was a problem because of old, loose rock from rock slides. The *Mountaineer*, No. 101, was extensively used on work trains on La Veta Pass. *Colorado Historical Society*

water could be transferred to the engine by a pump and hose arrangement. Fuel was shoveled from the box to a hillside close to the track then shoveled into the engine fuel box.

The Fairlee engine had one boiler, two copper fireboxes and was fired from the side. Each firebox had a double-sliding door with a water space of three inches between boxes. It had two throttles controlled by three levers, one of which reached over to the fireman's side so he could shut off the engine in an emergency. It was impossible to cross over the boiler in the cab since the throttle levers were on top of the boiler and there were numerous pipes and gauges.

When one engine was in forward motion, the other was in backward motion. The only way to tell which direction the engine was going to travel was to watch a little telltale. Whichever way that moved was the direction the engine would travel. At night, it was difficult to see the telltale.

The engine had a saddle tank. On the engineer's side were two water tanks, and on the fireman's side

DUMP MT FROM MULE SHOE 1403.

This rough picture is a manufacturer's plate for a combination baggage-mail car for the Denver & Rio Grande. Note the link and pin couplers, lack of air brakes, end door and the single axle trucks.

The *Mountaineer* was one of the first purchases for the D&RG, but it was a failure in road service, and it was put to work in construction service on old La Veta Pass. The double ended locomotive had a small water and fuel capacity. *Colorado Historical Society*

Engine #206 is at about Milepost 365 in Monero Canyon on the 24 degree curve—the sharpest on the Narrow Gauge; the little steamer appears all shined up for the occasion. *Colorado Historical Society*

were two coal bunkers. Neither of these were of sufficient capacity for protracted use.

In order to oil the engine's gears and rods, it was necessary to get underneath the engine. At roundhouses, the engine could be spotted over a pit. On the road, you had to find a hole under the track or dig one. D&RG water tanks were equipped with a counterbalanced spout that allowed water to flow into the engine tenders when pulled down, but this could not be done on the Fairlee. The tender was filled by using a hand pump on the engineer's side. It was a wet job and wasted a lot of water.

The *Mountaineer* was an operating headache. It is no surprise that no other railroads in the United States ever bought one. It was scrapped in 1883. Though the standard gauge Fairlee was not popular in the United States, it was very popular in Mexico.

The *Mountaineer* was probably never used west of Garland City when construction was resumed toward

Alamosa. Construction trains that worked toward Santa Fe or on the San Juan Extension to Durango were hauled by American-made, typical engines.

ENGINE NO. 206

One such typical engine was No. 206, which is seen in the photograph at a prominent location in Monero Canyon en route to what was then the railhead at Amargo, New Mexico. This location was at the sharpest curve on the Narrow Gauge and near a quarry where rock for building railroad culverts was produced. For about the first 10 years, this curve was classed as nearly 30 degrees. Finally, a powder crew was sent, and they blasted away enough of a rock face to reduce curvature to 24 degrees. Then, the curve was no tighter than many of those on the Silverton Branch.

In the photograph, the crew members perched on the cowcatcher of the diamond-stacked engine with its kerosene (coal oil) headlight could very well have been watching the men blast the curve.

175

D&RG #65 and crew pose for this exceptional picture; note the combination front headlight and number board, the large cabbage stack, the graceful lines of this machine—and the small boy in the engineer's side door. *Colorado Historical Society*

Standard gauge Engine #1069 at Helper, Utah is fired and ready to go. The date is in the 1920s.

Observation Cars

The D&RG's roster of 1904 includes a list of standard gauge passenger cars including three observation cars, Nos. 780, 781 and 782. The dimensions of the cars were:

Length	50 ft. 3^1/$_2$ in.
Width	9 ft. 9^1/$_2$ in.
Trucks	4-wheel
Seating capacity	72

In August 1910, the cars were re-numbered as Nos. 791, 792 and 793. The last roster they were listed in was the 1923 issue, but I am not sure whether they were in service.

The same rosters list three narrow gauge observation cars of the same conformation: No. 500, Royal Gorge; No. 501, Black Canyon; and No. 502, Argus. Except for seating capacity and dimensions, the cars are identical:

Length	35 ft. 11 in.
Width	8 ft. ^{5}/$_8$ in.
Trucks	4-wheel
Seating capacity	48 (Royal Gorge)
	52 (Others)

The standard gauge cars were hauled on the rear of regularly scheduled passenger trains so that passengers could view the Rocky Mountain scenery. It cost a passenger four bits (50¢) extra to ride one of these cars, and without doubt, Glenwood Canyon and the Royal Gorge were considered prime scenery worth 50¢ to have an unobstructed view.

The Narrow Gauge, Cumbres Pass, Marshall Pass, the Black Canyon and the Silverton Branch should have rated use of such cars, but the circumstances evolving from the MoPac-WesPac-D&RG (Missouri Pacific-Western Pacific-Denver & Rio Grande) financial manipulations forced the D&RG into bankruptcy. This left the D&RG in such financial straits that even normal track maintenance was not performed.

Six years after bankruptcy, the D&RG's physical plant was in a dangerous, almost inoperable, condition. A 1923-1924 inspection and evaluation study reported the lines as "thin, used-up rails, rotten ties, and inadequate ballast." The only portion of the D&RGW given any sort of a passing grade was the Marshall Pass segment.

The condition of the tracks and facilities may have contributed to the demise of the open observation cars use even before 1923. While still listed in the equipment portion of the 1923 roster, the observation cars may not have been serviceable. The same circumstance may have kept the narrow gauge observation cars from being used.

Engine #419, doubleheaded with a third engine ahead of the caboose on Cumbres Pass hauling a trainload of lumber. The locomotives are still using oil-burning headlights. The lumber was loaded in gondolas and coal dump cars using upright stakes and crossbound with lumber boards. This method was used until steel bands, flat cars and forklifts came into use. *Colorado Historical Society*

Engine #3701 delivered new at Burnham Shops with proud shop hands and officer. This engine gave them trouble, however.

At least for the purpose designed, both the standard and narrow gauge cars were well-built and gave many people the opportunity to view Colorado landscape they otherwise might have missed. Admittedly, the open construction was basically unsafe, and the cars were not good revenue producers.

Steam Engines

I was privileged to dispatch trains powered with steam ranging in size from C-Class (narrow gauge) through the L-105 (3700 series) and the L-97 (3800 series) of standard gauge.

During the late summer of 1954, I was trainmaster at Helper, Utah. For some reason, there was an extraordinary increase in coal production from the Carbon County area. Some days we moved 600 cars of coal over Soldier Summit, which was in addition to a healthy through business. Because of the work load, we were falling behind. We needed more motive power and manpower to alleviate the situation.

The lack of manpower was somewhat relieved by borrowing men from the Utah Railroad and other D&RGW divisions. For engine power, three of the 3600 series steam engines were activated and sent to Helper. For several reasons, including the lack of water and fuel supply and a reoccurrence of mechanical failures that showed up on the move from Grand Junction to Helper, none of these engines worked west of Helper. They were finally moved to Pueblo and scrapped at the Colorado Fuel & Iron steel mill.

The first Mallet on the Rio Grande apparently was Engine No. 3361. This engine was in service in November 1909 and was one of several units rebuilt from 0-6-6-0s to 2-6-6-0s. Other 3300s, renumbered from the old Class 458 (1000 series) to Class L-62, arrived in February 1910.

The L-95 (96), 3400 series in 1913 was followed by the 3500, 3600, 3700 and 3800 series. The 3600 series engines were our workhorses.

As times changed, so did the motive power on the Rio Grande:

	STEAM	DIESEL
1923	460	0
1940	281	0
1944	270	47
1955	46	232
1959	0	254

The only steam left on the Rio Grande by 1959 was on the Narrow Gauge, which had 22 locomotives. Unless you went to the Narrow Gauge, you had to listen to Klaxon horns sounding at every crossing. The loss of the steam whistle brings tears to my eyes. What sound in this world is more beautiful than the echoes of a steam whistle?

At Chama, leaving with a train bound for Cumbres Pass. Engine #417 is coupled to #207. Note the equipment is still lettered for the D&RG. The #417 was delivered from Baldwin in 1887. The engine's weight was 62,150 pounds; the #207 weighed in at 59,330 pounds. *Colorado Historical Society*

Locomotives that Powered Passenger Trains

Soon after World War I, it was apparent that improving conditions on the Narrow Gauge would increase passenger and freight business, and it was mandatory we acquire newer and larger motive power. In 1923, the Rio Grande purchased 10 locomotives from the American Locomotive Works and numbered them Engine Nos. 470 to 479. Their class designation was K-28, and they had a wheel configuration of 2-8-2.

The Class K-28 engines were referred to by narrow gaugers as the "Sport Model" because of their sleek, racy lines and snappy response to the throttle. Consequently, they were considered as the glamour girls of our fleet and used predominantly in powering passenger trains between Alamosa, Durango, Antonito and Santa Fe, and between Salida and Gunnison.

These K-28s were too heavy for branchline and lighter rail district service. Where they were used in daily service, a total of six of the Sport Models were used on scheduled passenger trains. The remaining four were utilized in freight service or as trade-outs when maintenance was necessary for any of those in passenger service.

The K-28s were so successful that an order for 10 more engines built to the same specifications and configurations was placed with Baldwin. They went into

Engine #476 with beautifully sculptured front headlight receives an underbody inspection from Rio Grande crew in Durango on August 28, 1955. This "Sport Model" was too heavy for branch-line service and was used for both freight and passenger service. *M.D. McCarter collection*

service in 1925 classed as K-36s and numbered 480 to 489. About the only difference between the K-36s and the K-28s was that the K-36s were heavier and produced a greater tractive effort. They were used extensively on districts where rail weight was capable of carrying them safely.

STANDARD GAUGE

Increasing business on the standard gauge also required larger power, and the Rio Grande chose to retire most of the C-41 Class locomotives. Of those retired, the 10 in the best condition were modified to operate on the Narrow Gauge. These modified engines were classed as K-37s and numbered 490 to

499. Between 1928 and 1930, they were placed into service as the modifications were completed on each. They were good freight haulers, but they were never as popular as the Sport Models or the K-36s.

At the beginning of World War II, the Army took over seven of the K-28s for use in Alaska where the White Pass and Yukon Railroad was renovated to haul military supplies from Skagway to Whitehorse, which were then transhipped to trucks for movement to Fairbanks. Engine Nos. 473, 476 and 478 continued to be used on the Rio Grande for passenger service.

Passenger service on the Narrow Gauge was discontinued on the Santa Fe Branch between Salida and Gunnison and Alamosa and Durango. By February 1951, the only passenger service on the Narrow Gauge was for the summer and fall sightseeing excursions between Durango and Silverton. The Silverton Branch eventually was sold to Charles Bradshaw, who continues to operate it as a tourist attraction. Renamed as the Durango-Silverton Railroad, it is very successful. The three K-28s were included in the sale and are still in service.

Narrow gauge railroaders like other Westerners apply nicknames to people and equipment. Prior to the arrival of the K-28s, the heaviest engines in service were Class K-27, Nos. 450 to 464. Traveling down the track, they had a peculiar motion that resembled the motion of the aquatic bird called a mud hen. That was the appellation given the K-27s, and employees never referred to them by any other name.

About the time the K-28s arrived, automobile manufacturers were designing sportier cars rather than the square and bulky family cars. "Sport Cars" were built lower, sleeker and with more power. The first K-28s were hardly in service before they were being called Sport Models. And, they truly were.

ENGINE NO. 802

During the summer and fall vegetable shipping season and the fall livestock movement, we occasionally needed an additional steam engine to move business over La Veta Pass.

The most common engine used to do this was a T-29 (700 series), which powered Trains 15 and 16 (later, Nos. 115 and 116) from Pueblo to Alamosa. Sometimes a 800 series P-44 was used.

This train arrived at Alamosa 5:45 a.m. To our advantage, there was an eastbound passenger train that was not scheduled to leave Alamosa until 9:30 p.m., which meant that there were 15 hours and 45 minutes in which we could use that locomotive and still have it ready for passenger service.

The 90-mile round trip from Alamosa to Fir at the summit of La Veta Pass took six hours, which included the preparation and departure time for the passenger engine. This gave us plenty of time to use it on the freight movements.

Stately Rio Grande standard gauge 4-6-0 #784 of the T-29 Class pulls into the Montrose station with a passenger train on June 8, 1951. The locomotive looks slightly soiled. *Denver Public Library, Western History Section*

A 4-6-2 of the P-44 Class rests quietly near the roundhouse at Alamosa, tires and cylinders all painted, as is smokebox and exhaust stack. With a full tender of coal, this standard gauge engine is ready to hit the high iron. *Denver Public Library, Western History Section*

The P-44 had a tractive power of 45,000 pounds; the T-29 was rated at 30,000 pounds. We predominantly used the M-67/69 engines (1500 series), which had a tractive power of 67,000 pounds, and the L-95 engines (3400 series), which had a tractive power of 95,000 pounds, over La Veta Pass.

On the heaviest part of the grade, Sierra to Fir, the M-67/69 was rated for 975 tons of freight; the L-95 was rated for 1,275 tons. No tonnage rating was specified for either the T-29 or P-44. Empirically, we used 500 tons as a rating—usually five carloads of vegetables or seven cars of livestock.

Occasionally, if we were pressed for time, we would drop the engine down to Sierra (6 miles) to help a second train to Fir. This required another two hours and was risky, but we did what had to be done.

Another trick was to move a string of badly needed refrigerator or livestock cars to Fir from La Veta on a turn, set them out and let the passenger engine, using a deadheaded caboose and train crew, bring them to Alamosa on the descending grade, which made the T-29 or P-44 as useful as the larger engines.

ENGINE NO. 784

The Rio Grande never had any "high wheelers" in its fleet as some flat land railroads had, and the closest the D&RG came to such engines were the ones purchased in 1896. These were classified as T-29s and carried a series of numbers that began with 700. Roster No. 10 issued in 1916 listed 76 locomotives on the D&RG and 11 on the RGW with numbers in the 700s. The lowest is 700, and the highest is 793.

The 700s were the first locomotives on the Rio Grande to bring the total locomotive weight to close to 100 tons. Until then, the heaviest was less than 75 tons. Engine No. 700 was rated as 149,065 pounds and gradually increased in weight. Engine No. 793 had a total locomotive weight of 184,000 pounds. The same year the Rio Grande received its first 2-6-6-

2 Mallets, the last of the 700s were put into service. This was in 1910.

Until the T-29s arrived, driver diameter was between 40 to 44 inches. The T-29s built between 1896 and 1889 had 56-inch drivers, and later models had 60-inch drivers. There is some information from old D&RG records that all the rear drivers on the T-29s had diameters three to seven inches larger than the lead drivers.

Pre-1902 cylinders were 20 x 26 inches; later, they were 21 x 26 inches. Regardless of which company built the T-29 and P-44 engines, they had a uniform configuration and structure.

The 700s were designed and built for passenger train service in mountainous territory. The original locomotives were so well-built that no major changes in either the design or construction were made. They were used almost entirely to power the standard gauge main line and some branch line passenger trains until the advent of the K-29 (1200 series) and M-67 (1500 series).

Many were still in service or restored to active service and used for handling regular and troop trains during World War II. The overall performance of the 700s was on par with the beloved and respected K-28 narrow gauge engine, the "Sport Model." After logging hundreds of thousands, and possibly millions, of trouble-free miles, Engine No. 784, the last of the 700s, was scrapped in June 1952.

Referring to the 700s as T-29s was not quite an accurate designation. Within the number series for various Interstate Commerce Commission regulations and for mechanical reasons, the classifications varied. Some were T-28s, some were T-29s, and others were T-31s. But everyone knew that if you spoke of a T-29, you referred to a 700.

Those 700s did not have drivers as tall as those on Casey Jones' engine, but to us on the Rio Grande, they were "high wheelers."

			MILES				Time Departed	Time Arrived	Hours on Road	Delayed Time
Train	FROM	TO	Regular	Helper	Light	Mixed				
X	Ridgway	Dallas Divide	14				1:15	4:05	2:50	1:05
X	Dallas Divide	Ridgway	13				4:25	5:25	1	0

THE DENVER AND RIO GRANDE R. R. CO.

Engine No. 10 Date 6-14 -19-16 191___

Called for Train E X to leave at 1:10 PM Overtime claimed 1

G. Talbot 405 Engineer.

H P Walford 405 Fireman.

Always Explain "Work."
Always Explain Delays on Back.

 # Acknowledgements

So many people over the years have contributed information, photographs, recollections and stories for my use in writing about railroads, especially the Rio Grande, it is impossible to extend individual acknowledgements to each. But to all of you, wherever you are, you know you have helped. I want to express my heartfelt gratitude to all of you. Those who have been especially helpful with this book are:

Orvil Benson
Leonard J. Berstein
The Denver Public Library—Western History Section
J. Gordon Low
M.D. McCarter
James (Jim) Ozment
R.W. (Bob) Richardson
Dr. Richard Severance
The State Historical Society of Colorado
Jackson C. Thode

My appreciation also goes to my publisher, Donald Heimburger, for his support, ideas and incentive to keep digging for more pictures, more data and accuracy. There were many times when a hunting or fishing trip would have been more to my liking.

My continued admiration for the staff of Heimburger House Publishing, especially Donald's wife, Marilyn, the best layout artist and indexer in the industry.

With such help from so many, even an Arkansas hillbilly can turn out a book. Thanks again to all.

Bibliography

1. Robert G. Athearn. *Rebel of the Rockies,* 1962.

2. Lucius Beebe. Bulletin No. 67A, *Narrow Gauge Railroads of Colorado.*

3. Lucius Beebe. *Narrow Gauge In The Rockies,* 1958.

4. Herbert O. Brayer. *Early Financing Of The Denver & Rio Grande Railway,* 1949.

5. Colorado Historical Society. *The Georgetown Loop,* 1986.

6. Colorado State Historical Society Museum, Denver. Numerous files, reference books and archival materials.

7. Colorado State Geological Survey. Bulletins Nos. 1 to 6, various years.

8. Cubar Associates. *Crofutt's Guide Of Colorado,* 1966.

9. Denver Public Library. Various reference books, files and archives.

10. Denver & Rio Grande Summaries Of Equipment. Various years.

11. Perry Eberhart. *Guide To The Colorado Ghost Towns,* 1959.

12. Vardis Fisher and Opal Laurel Holmes. *Gold Rushes And Mining Camps Of The Early American West,* 1968.

13. Leroy R. Hafen. *Colorado And Its People, Vols. I and II,* 1948.

14. Donald J. Heimburger. *Rio Grande Steam Locomotives, Standard Gauge,* 1981.

15. Rossiter Johnson. *Campfires and Battlefields (Civil War),* 1967.

16. ——. Official Roster, The Denver & Rio Grande Railroad System, No. 10, April 1, 1916.

17. ——. Official Roster, The Denver & Rio Grande Western Railroad System, No. 11, April 11, 1923.

18. ——. Railway Guides, various issues.

19. Marshall Sprague. *The Great Gates,* 1964.

20. Jackson C. Thode. *A Century Of Passenger Trains,* 1972.

21. Carl Ubbelohde. *A Colorado History,* 1965.

APPENDIX

DENVER & RIO GRANDE RAILROAD SYSTEM
(Report of October, 1914)
*with annotations of changes or comments in subsequent years

PHYSICAL CONDITION

The total trackage owned or operated by the Company, including second, passing, side and spur tracks, is 3,617 miles. Of this there are

standard gauge main line and branches	2,088	miles.
Narrow gauge main line and branches	820	"
Standard gauge sidings and spurs	615	"
Narrow gauge sidings and spurs	94	"

The foregoing includes 208 miles of standard gauge second main track.

GRADES

The profile of the main line between Denver and Ogden is attached hereto.

On the standard gauge line to Alamosa, a maximum grade of 3% must be surmounted by trains moving over La Veta Pass in the direction of Alamosa, and 2.5% grade in the opposite direction. On both the Durango and Marshall Pass narrow gauge lines 4% grades prevail, and elsewhere, by reason of the mountainous nature of the country, the gradients are equally as great.

CURVATURE

Much of the alignment contains curvature which can be reduced or entirely eliminated at a moderate expense, which if done would reduce maintenance cost and permit increase in the speed of trains. On the main line between Canon City and Salida, in the Canons of the Arkansas River, between Salida and Tennessee Pass, and between Minturn and Glenwood, the curvature is frequent and of especial prominence. At each of these places 10 degree curves are prevalent, and 12 degree and over are sometimes employed.

RAIL

Between Denver and Salt Lake the main track contains 657 miles of 85-lb. rail and 86 miles of 90-lb. rail. Between Salt Lake and Ogden (37 miles) 75-lb. rail is used in main line, except for the distance of six-hundredths of a mile in Ogden Yard, where there is 65-lb. rail. The rail on the main line is in a reasonably fair condition, and the purchase each year of 10,000 tons of first quality rail for renewals will be sufficient to maintain the tracks safe for operation.

*System mileage as of December 31, 1916, was:

Standard gauge main line and branches	1,942	miles
Narrow gauge main line and branches	798	"
Standard gauge sidings and spurs	643	"
Narrow gauge sidings and spurs	97	"

*The foregoing includes 206 miles of standard gauge second main track.

ICING FACILITIES

There are in service 39 ice houses of varying size, having a total capacity of 102,596 tons. The Company owns ice ponds at Pando, Colton, Palmer Lake and Gorgoza, their relative importance being in the order named. During the winter of 1913-1914, 63,500 tons of ice were harvested and stored in the houses, which, with what was left in the houses from the previous year, was sufficient to fill them. The more important icing stations are located at:

	Capacity Tons
Denver	10,000
Burnham	3,700
Pueblo	15,000
Salida	3,000
Pando	4,000
Minturn	5,000
Grand Junction	21,000
Delta	10,000
Colton	4,000
Provo	4,000
Salt Lake	2,400
Ogden	1,800
Alamosa	2,000
Durango	1,000

A total of 9,433 tons of artificial ice was purchased this year at Denver, Colorado Springs, Pueblo, Canon City, Glenwood, Grand Junction, Salt Lake and Durango, the amount stored not having been sufficient to provide for the season's requirements, which, owing to an unusually heavy fruit crop, were greater than anticipated.

Necessities for more improved icing facilities are increasingly manifest as horticulture develops in tributary territory and interline movement of perishable freight increases. With the exception of that at Minturn, none of the ice plants is entirely modern in appliances or conveniences; and greater efficiency and a substantial saving in cost of operation can be effected by the expenditure of moderate sums for reconstructing the defective houses and providing mechanical appliances to facilitate the loading of ice into the houses and the icing of cars.

Experience has shown it desirable to store larger quantities of ice at higher altitudes, where loss by melting is at a minimum, and where refrigerator cars can be iced and quickly transported to the place where they are to be loaded. Pando and Colton, where important ice ponds are located, offer superior advantages for storing ice to be used in the Grand River Valley and Provo Valley, respectively, and at these places it is proposed to construct additional houses and tracks where a large number of refrigerator cars can be assembled for the season's requirements.

At all of the more important icing stations large sums can be saved by the installation of improved machinery for handling ice, thereby reducing the time required to ice cars and saving large sums heretofore paid out for labor and lost by shrinkage. For improved appliances and enlarged facilities for storage, the following appropriations are recommended:

	Period	Expenses	R. & R.	Total
Pando and Colton	First	$10,000	$45,000	$55,000
Machinery	First	5,000	15,000	20,000
Miscellaneous Improvements	Second		25,000	25,000
Miscellaneous Improvements	Third		15,000	15,000
Miscellaneous Improvements	Fourth		10,000	10,000
Total		$15,000	$110,000	$125,000

Of the foregoing, $40,000 should hbe expended on improvement of ice handling facilities, which will produce an annual savings of 30%. The remainder, $85,000, should be expended for ice pond facilities and increased storage. The necessity for the latter expenditure is dependent upon the business increasing and will not be made unless so justified.

AUTOMATIC BLOCK SIGNALS

It will be noted in statements covering estimates of expenditures recommended, that large sums are proposed for installation of automatic block signals on the main line between Denver and Salt Lake, the disbursements to run through three periods, and to aggregate $1,335,000. Popular sentiment is now strongly in favor of the application of such safety devices, and it is problable that their installation on all important lines will soon be compelled by legislative action. Their use would possibly influence many passengers to patronize the Denver & Rio Grande who otherwise would travel via other routes, but it cannot be demonstrated that the expenditure for installation would bring important saving in operating expenses. Until pressure is brought to bear through legislative or regulative bodies, it is not the intention to apply the appropriation for this improvement except through the Royal Gorge and between Helper and Solder Summit.

*No progress has been made on the authorization or installation of block signals, although the installation of safety appliances of this character is a question which receives the attention of State and Federal Authorities, who, at different times, have strongly urged their installation on other lines.

*On heavy traffic train districts, especially those having through passenger service, automatic block signals are an efficient aid to the prompt, safe and economical movement of both passenger and freight trains.

SOUTH FORK TO DURANGO

In Southwestern Colorado, Northwestern New Mexico and the extension of Montezuma Valley in Utah, the agricultural possiblities are about as follows, land on Indian Reservations excluded:

Now included in irrigation systems..	176,000 acres
Capable of development by irrigation	916,000 acres
Can be profitably farmed without irrigation	130,000 acres
Total agricultural area	1,222,000 acres

There are 93,000 acres now under cultivation.

The land is fertile, water is abundant, and the climate healthful and agreeable. Capital is needed to develop the country, but experience teaches that capital cannot be secured in large amounts for the development of territory entirely dependent upon narrow gauge service.

It is recommended that, as soon as the financial situation will permit, a standard gauge line be built to Durango by the construction of a new line between South Fork and Juanita, and the standardizing of the narrow gauge line from Juanita to Durango. Such line is needed to protect the territory against invasion by the Atchison, Topeka & Santa Fe and Southern Pacific, as well as to hasten the development of the country to be traversed. There is strong probability that large investments will be made to immediately irrigate and colonize the lands when assurances are given that the improved transportation facilities will be provided. It is believed the operation of the suggested new line will be profitable from the start and that the development of the country will furnish large additional revenues to the Company's earnings. It is estimated that there are at this time in the Uncompahgre, North Fork and Grand River Valleys between Palisade and Mack a total of 135,580 acres of cultivated land out of 239,655 acres under ditch.

Estimated cost, South Fork to Juanita	$3,300,000
Estimated cost, Juanita to Durango	1,200,000
Improvement of shop facilities, Alamosa and Durango	300,000
Total	$4,800,000

To assist in the agricultural development of this region and, at the same time, protect the interests of the Company against possible competitors, it will probably be necessary to build a standard gauge line following the San Juan River from Arboles to Farmington and from Farmington for a distance of 10 to 15 miles down the San Juan Valley; also from Farmington via the La Plata Valley and Mancos into the Montezuma Valley.

No estimate of cost can now be given and, at this time, it is not believed probable that necessity for the line will arise before expiration of the Fourth Period.

The statement next attached demonstrates that present narrow gauge operations, while conducted at less than heretofore, are a source of serious loss to the Company.

The proposed standard gauge line to Durango, when built, can be operated for 70% or less of its gross revenues.

Narrow Gauge Lines: The operation of the Company's narrow gauge lines is unduly expensive. Suitable power and freight equipment have not been furnished and track has not been improved to permit the use of heavier power and car equipment. As a result, narrow gauge operation costs show the following unsatisfactory record:

	Fiscal Year 1912		Fiscal Year 1913		Fiscal Year 1914		Fiscal Year 1915		Fiscal Year 1916	
	Operating Revenue	% Operating Revenue	Operating Revenue	% Operating Revenue	Operating Revenue	% Operating Revenue	Operating Revenue	% Operating Revenue	Operating Revenue	% Operating Revenue
Freight	$1,309,420.21	68.78	$1,343,414.79	68.19	$1,249,271.72	66.86	$1,165,872.73	67.34	$1,304,966.63	69.01
Passenger	428,530.88	22.51	453,428.79	23.01	456,814.25	24.45	388,632.32	22.44	406,299.71	21.49
Mail	77,184.21	4.05	78,485.85	3.98	81,120.11	4.34	82,035.40	4.74	74,014.57	3.91
Express	56,096.71	2.95	58,093.49	2.95	45,687.51	2.45	48,361.16	2.79	61,283.98	3.24
Miscellaneous	32,616.16	1.71	36,882.92	1.87	35,582.21	1.90	46,515.19	2.69	44,410.70	2.35
Total Operating Revenue	$1,903,848.17	100.00	$1,970,305.84	100.00	$1,868,475.80	100.00	$1,731,416.80	100.00	$1,890,975.49	100.00
	Expenses		Expenses		Expenses		Expenses		Expenses	
Maintenance of Way & Str	$ 737,023.35	38.71	$ 637,771.97	32.37	$ 572,671.75	30.65	$ 424,107.38	24.49	$ 466,862.52	24.69
Maintenance Equipment	459,680.65	24.13	545,816.07	27.70	450,889.20	24.13	415,502.15	24.00	447,575.19	23.67
Traffic Expenses	70,848.04	3.72	63,868.49	3.24	60,605.53	3.24	65,602.92	3.79	69,228.83	3.66
Transportation	886,508.54	46.56	876,597.23	44.49	807,900.15	43.24	770,103.42	44.48	861,274.89	45.55
General	75,021.59	3.94	84,122.56	4.27	82,057.51	4.39	89,907.82	5.20	105,615.29	5.48
Miscellaneous	—	—	—	—	—	—	10,738.77	.62	11,722.27	.62
Transportation for Investment-Cr.	—	—	—	—	—	—	374.45 CR	.02	—	—
Total Operating Expenses	$2,229,082.05	117.08	$2,208,176.32	112.07	$1,974,124.14	105.65	$1,775,588.01	102.55	$1,960,278.99	103.67
Deficit	$ 325,233.88	17.08	$ 237,870.48	12.07	$ 105,648.34	5.65	$ 44,171.21	2.55	$ 69,303.50	3.67

SALIDA TO MONTROSE

The line between Salida and Montrose is in better physical condition than is that of the other narrow gauge branches. The track is laid with heavier steel, which permits the use of the heaviest narrow gauge equipment over the steep grades between Salida and Gunnison. Consequently, operating costs are lower than in other narrow gauge territory, which emphasizes the desirability of either reconstructing the narrow gauge lines and purchasing new power and equipment, or changing to standard gauge, which can be more economically operated.

Ninety-seven out of the 112 narrow gauge engines owned by the Company were purchased in 1887 and prior to that year; 112 out of 120 passenger cars owned were purchased prior to 1900. Unless large portions of the narrow gauge lines are changed to standard gauge, thus releasing equipment for service elsewhere, the Company will be compelled to purchase additional narrow gauge equipment within three years. Transfer of freight from and to narrow gauge cars cost from 10 to 18 cents per ton.

It has been estimated that the cost to standard gauge the Marshall Pass Line between Salida and Montrose, together with the Crested Butte, Ouray and Alamosa Branches, is $2,650,000. Such an estimate contemplates reducing the maximum rate of curve to 20 degrees without any reduction in rate of grade.

*It is necessary that Denver reach an early decision as to whether operation of the narrow gauge lines shall be perpetuated, or whether these lines as have further traffic development possibilities shall be relocated and reconstructed to provide economical standard gauge operations.

*Undoubtedly rehabilitation of narrow gauge lines and the purchase of new narrow gauge equipment will afford some economy in operation. Such action will not, however, contribute to any appreciable extent toward minimizing the cost of standardization when it becomes ultimately necessary, nor will it aid the development and growth of the territories traversed as will standard gauge lines. On the other hand, the installation of standard gauge operations will undoubtedly stimulate the development of the country and offers opportunity for continued future use of materials and equipment released on main lines; likewise opportunity for construction of the best of narrow gauge equipment on remaining narrow gauge lines where further traffic development is not anticipated for a decade or more.

*Initial observation and analysis of narrow gauge operations is apt to lead to the conclusion that such lines are adequate for present and near future requirements of their territory. Further observation and analysis of the conditions governing the investment of capital and colonizing and industrial development leads to the ultimate conclusion that certain of the narrow gauge territories can be profitably standardized both for increased revenues and economic operation.

*There is no doubt that a decided prejudice exists against narrow gauge lines and against the country served by narrow gauge lines. Capital is not forthcoming for irrigation projects or for industrial development in territories where it is understood that narrow gauge service will prevail in the future, and colonists are loath to establish permanent homes in such districts, even though the country is susceptible to profitable agricultural development.

EQUIPMENT

The Company owns 617 engines, of which 162 are designed for passenger service, 412 for freight and 43 for switching service. Included in these are 36 engines purchased during the past two years direct from the manufacturers, of which 6 are Pacific type for passenger service, 16 Mallet and 14 Mikado engines for freight service, also one consolidation freight engine secured with the purchase of the Spring Canyon Coal Company. These purchases have increased the average tractive power for all locomotives 2,497 pounds, resulting in an average tractive effort of 18,621 pounds per engine.

Of the engines owned, it has been recommended that 20 be scrapped for the reason that the cost to put them into good condition would equal about 60% of their book value. These are all of light weight and were purchased from 1881 to 1890.

The condition of power on June 30, 1910, as compared with June 30, 1914, is as follows:

	Good	Fair	Poor	Out of Service
June 30, 1910	46%	18%	13%	23%
June 30, 1914	50%	26.9%	5.6%	17.1%

Of the engines out of service in 1914, 19% are recommended to be scrapped.

The tractive force of the engines for mountain grades is entirely too light, and in recommendations for expenditures during the first period provision has been made for the purchase of larger power to be used on the heavy grades, as follows:

12 Mountain type passenger engines at $30,000	$ 360,000
5 Centipede ” helping ” ” 48,000	240,000
33 2-10-2 ” freight ;; ” 45,000	1,485,000
Total	$2,085,000

The operation of these engines, together with the efficient use on either districts of the power which they will replace, will effect an operating saving of about $500,000 per year.

Additional locomotives are for the purpose of securing power adapted to the property and thereby reducing cost of transportation. It is not to be expected that the Denver & Rio Grande, with its heavy grades, will receive any higher rate per ton mile than its neighbors with low grade lines, and it must, therefore, equip itself with power that will equalize grades and permit of as low a cost for transportation as that of its competitors.

The Company owns and has in operation 457 passenger cars, via:

Passenger cars	239
Combination cars	39
Dining cars	23
Baggage, Express & Mail Cars	156

Standard Gauge Operations			1914	1915	1916	Average	% Increase Over Narrow Gauge
Stations between Grand Junction and Montrose	)	Passenger	$107,514	$ 94,573	$ 92,639	$ 98,242	7.2
	)	Freight Forwarded	221,450	256,340	236,237	238,009	189.0
	)	Freight Received	179,811	165,053	174,451	173,105	90.1
	)	Total	$508,775	$ 515,966	$503,327	$509,356	77.4
	)	% Increase or Decrease over 1914		1.4	-1.1	0.1	
Stations between Delta and Somerset, excluding Delta	)	Passenger	$ 28,382	$ 29,174	$ 26,472	$ 28,009	42.0
	)	Freight Forwarded	309,716	430,880	289,371	343,322	121.0
	)	Freight Received	82,922	76,035	71,533	76,830	11.0
	)	Total	$421,020	$ 536,089	$387,376	$448,161	83.3
	)	% Increase or Decrease over 1914		27.3	-8.0	6.4	
Totals of Above	)	Passenger	$135,897	$ 123,747	$119,111	$126,251	42.5
	)	Freight Forwarded	531,166	687,220	525,608	581,331	144.5
	)	Freight Received	262,733	241,088	245,984	249,935	21.7
	)	Total	$929,796	$1,052,055	$890,703	$957,517	80.1
	)	% Increase or Decrease over 1914		13.1	-4.2	2.9	

Narrow Gauge Operations			1904	1905	1906	3 Year Average	
Stations between Grand Junction and Montrose	)	Passenger	$ 59,145	$ 64,642	$ 82,909	$ 68,898	
	)	Freight Forwarded	76,201	95,131	75,160	82,164	
	)	Freight Received	114,041	137,954	156,082	136,026	
	)	Total	$249,387	$297,727	$ 314,151	$ 287,090	
	)	% Increase or Decrease over 1904		19.4	25.9	15.1	
Stations between Delta and Somerset, excluding Delta	)	Passenger	$ 16,533	$ 19,944	$ 22,528	$ 19,668	
	)	Freight Forwarded	192,273	114,316	159,983	155,524	
	)	Freight Received	65,253	76,643	65,885	69,261	
	)	Total	$274,059	$210,903	$248,396	$244,453	
	)	% Increase or Decrease over 1904		-23.0	-9.3	-10.8	
Totals of Above	)	Passenger	$ 75,678	$ 84,586	$105,437	$ 88,567	
	)	Freight Forwarded	268,474	209,447	235,143	237,688	
	)	Freight Received	179,294	214,597	221,967	205,287	
	)	Total	$523,446	$508,630	$562,547	$531,542	
	)	% Increase or Decrease over 1914		-2.9	7.4	1.5	

INDEX

191